Y0-BDD-122

Understanding

Frankenstein

Don Nardo

LUCENT
BOOKS®

THOMSON
™
GALE

San Diego • Detroit • New York • San Francisco • Cleveland
New Haven, Conn. • Waterville, Maine • London • Munich

THOMSON
✳ ™
GALE

On cover: In the famous 1931 film *Frankenstein,* Boris Karloff appears as the creature brought to life by Dr. Frankenstein.

LIBRARY OF CONGRESS CATALOGING-IN-PUBLICATION DATA

Nardo, Don, 1947–
   Frankenstein / by Don Nardo.
     p. cm. — (Understanding great literature)
Summary: Discusses Mary Shelley's sources of ideas for the compelling plot, well-developed characters, and universal themes of "Frankenstein," which have led to its enduring popularity.
   Includes bibliographical references (p.   ) and index.
   ISBN 1-59018-147-6 (hardback : alk. paper)
   1. Shelley, Mary Wollstonecraft, 1797–1851. Frankenstein—Juvenile literature.
2. Frankenstein (Fictitious character)—Juvenile literature. [1. Shelley, Mary Wollstonecraft, 1797–1851. Frankenstein. 2. English literature—History and criticism.] I. Title II. Series.
PR5397.F73N37 2003
823' .7—dc21

                                                                    2002012560

Y823.7
Nardo
Mar. 1, 2004

Printed in the United States of America

Contents

FOREWORD

"Except for a living man, there is nothing more wonderful than a book!" wrote the widely respected nineteenth-century teacher and writer Charles Kingsley. A book, he continued, "is a message to us from human souls we never saw. And yet these [books] arouse us, terrify us, teach us, comfort us, open our hearts to us as brothers." There are many different kinds of books, of course; and Kingsley was referring mainly to those containing literature—novels, plays, short stories, poems, and so on. In particular, he had in mind those works of literature that were and remain widely popular with readers of all ages and from many walks of life.

Such popularity might be based on one or several factors. On the one hand, a book might be read and studied by people in generation after generation because it is a literary classic, with characters and themes of universal relevance and appeal. Homer's epic poems, the *Iliad* and the *Odyssey*, Chaucer's *Canterbury Tales*, Shakespeare's *Hamlet* and *Romeo and Juliet*, and Dickens's *A Christmas Carol* fall into this category. Some popular books, on the other hand, are more controversial. Mark Twain's *Huckleberry Finn* and J.D. Salinger's *The Catcher in the Rye*, for instance, have their legions of devoted fans who see them as great literature; while others view them as less than worthy because of their racial depictions, profanity, or other factors.

Still another category of popular literature includes realistic modern fiction, including novels such as Robert Cormier's *I Am the Cheese* and S.E. Hinton's *The Outsiders*. Their keen social insights and sharp character portrayals have consistently reached out to and captured the imaginations of many teenagers and young adults; and for this reason they are often assigned and studied in schools.

These and other similar works have become the "old standards" of the literary scene. They are the ones that people most often read, discuss, and study; and each has, by virtue of its content, critical success, or just plain longevity, earned the right to be the subject of a book examining its content. (Some, of course, like the *Iliad* and *Hamlet*, have been the subjects of numerous books already; but their literary stature is so lofty that there can never be too many books about them!) For millions of readers and students in one generation after another, each of these works becomes, in a sense, an adventure in appreciation, enjoyment, and learning.

The main purpose of Lucent's Understanding Great Literature series is to aid the reader in that ongoing literary adventure. Each volume in the series focuses on a single literary work that a majority of critics and teachers view as a classic and/or that is widely studied and discussed in schools. A typical volume first tells why the work in question is important. Then follow detailed overviews of the author's life, the work's historical background, its plot, its characters, and its themes. Numerous quotes from the work, as well as by critics and other experts, are interspersed throughout and carefully documented with footnotes for those who wish to pursue further research. Also included is a list of ideas for essays and other student projects relating to the work, an appendix of literary criticisms and analyses by noted scholars, and a comprehensive annotated bibliography.

The great nineteenth-century American poet Henry David Thoreau once quipped: "Read the best books first, or you may not have a chance to read them at all." For those who are reading or about to read the "best books" in the literary canon, the comprehensive, thorough, and thoughtful volumes of the Understanding Great Literature series are indispensable guides and sources of enrichment.

Not One but Many Frankensteins

Today nearly everyone, regardless of age, background, or educational level, is familiar with the name Frankenstein. It has come to symbolize the creation of life in a laboratory rather than by the hand of God or natural evolution. It has also become a metaphor for the idea of science run amok, of dangerous experiments that tamper in areas of questionable morality. And it conjures up images of misshapen, half-human monsters terrorizing and killing innocent people before finally being apprehended and killed by the authorities.

Indeed, a seemingly endless array of popular movies, TV shows, comic books, video games, and other media venues perpetuate instantly recognizable scenes associated with Frankenstein. Among them are futuristic-looking labs that are atmospherically lit and packed with strange machines generating arcs of electricity. In many such scenes, a crazed-looking researcher, often assisted by a hunchback or other deformed person, hovers over a dead body lying on a table. Using various mysterious means, the "mad" scientist animates the corpse with life. Soon the creature stirs, opens its eyes, and looks around with a mixture of fear and confusion. And inevitably it turns on its creator, who learns the folly of meddling in "God's domain." Meanwhile, having killed again and again, the creature is chased by angry villagers (or city folk, or soldiers, or dogs, depending on the setting), cornered, and killed. Yet this is not the end of the typical Frankenstein story. More often than not, the monster is later resurrected, either by the efforts of another mad scientist or by accident, and once more threatens the lives of decent people.

Dark, Compelling Themes

It is a fascinating commentary on the human imagination, as well as popular tastes and demands for fiction depicting

This large, gothic-looking lab was constructed for a 1993 TV version of Frankenstein.

monstrosity, murder, and mayhem, that most of the modern depictions of Frankenstein bear only a partial resemblance to the story that inspired them. That story originated as the plot of a novel titled *Frankenstein: Or, the Modern Prometheus,* first published in 1818. And the author, many people today are surprised to learn, was a teenage girl. Mary Shelley was the daughter and wife of famous and controversial English writers, and she became no less controversial herself with her tale of the

Mary Shelley was still in her teens when she penned Frankenstein, *then seen as a tale of unspeakable horror.*

artificial creation of life. That concept was seen as disturbing, even horrifying at the time. "It produced shock and bewilderment," comments noted drama critic Christopher Small.

> When it first appeared its newness may fairly be called staggering. . . . There was something monstrous about its central idea that produced the typical reactions of people confronted with a *lusus naturae,* a breach in the accepted order of things.[1]

The book's controversial main theme was not the only attribute that made it endure. The author's effective use of atmosphere and skillful development of character and secondary themes helped make the novel one of the best and most influential works of the English Romantic period of fiction writing. The reading public of the early nineteenth century was fascinated by and drawn to Shelley's exploration of some crucial human and social concepts. These included the agony of alienation and becoming a social outcast; the terrible cycle of murder and revenge; the conflict between human intellect and emotion; the dark potential of misusing scientific advances; the inborn fear of things strange and ugly; the toll of solitude and loneliness; and the proper relationship between humans and God. Moreover, the author developed these themes within the compelling framework of the then-popular gothic (dark, mysterious, twisted) setting and style.

The Heart of Her Vision

The original book has no hunchbacked assistant or angry villagers, and the "monster" is not a dim-witted, unfeeling, or evil beast. These and other now familiar images were added in the many subsequent literary and film adaptations. Yet nearly all the later versions of *Frankenstein* have retained the main characters and central concepts of Mary Shelley's original: A human scientist named Frankenstein creates life in a lab, boldly challenging one of God's sovereign rights. And because of factors the man did not foresee and cannot control, the results are tragic for himself, his family, and his friends.

These few characters and central concepts not only laid the groundwork for later speculative fiction involving scientific themes (including the science fiction genre) but also immediately gave birth to a relentless onslaught of stage, film, and other adaptations that has not abated, or even slowed, to this day. As University of Northumbria scholar Peter Hutchings suggests, "There is no such thing as *Frankenstein,* there are only *Frankensteins,* as the text is ceaselessly rewritten, reproduced, refilmed and redesigned."[2] It is sometimes difficult, therefore, to discern which ideas originated in the novel and which were later added to the growing "Frankenstein mythos"—that is, the accumulation of various characters, themes, symbols, and story lines based directly or loosely on the original, all circulating in the public consciousness.

Yet the growth of this mythos and multiple Frankensteins neither diminishes the importance and power of the original nor condemns the later adaptations as mere rip-offs. In all probability, Mary Shelley would have liked the idea of her central characters and concepts remaining alive indefinitely in other venues. The subsequent alterations in the story line and the addition of new characters can be seen as natural responses to subsequent changes in society and technology. The important point is that the heart of her vision lives on, and probably always will, in the cultural mind. In the words of Wheeler W. Dixon, of the University of Nebraska,

> The essence of her novel survives the many emendations [changes and corrections] made to her plot. Even the assembly line of screenwriters [over the years] . . . could not [ignore] her central themes: the creation of a being from the remnants of human beings; the questions of birth, life, and death and of the immortality of the soul. . . . Although the definitive [best, most im-

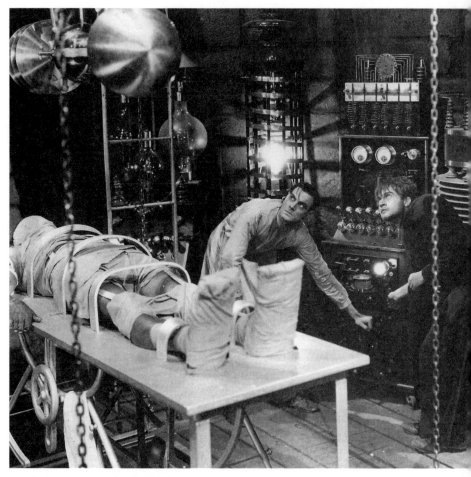

In the first sound film of Frankenstein *(1931), Frankenstein and his deformed assistant prepare to animate the creature with the spark of life.*

portant] *Frankenstein* may be in the future, all the films . . . may serve as keys to the novel, as seen through the mirror of Hollywood invention or through a faithful adaptation of the original text. The list of these films demonstrates that when the task is approached with taste and skill, it is possible to transfer the gothic sensibility without compromise—an endeavor I feel certain Mary Wollstonecraft Shelley, visionary that she was, would enthusiastically have approved.[3]

CHAPTER ONE

The Life and Influences of Mary Shelley

From an early age, Mary Shelley, one of the most famous and popular English novelists of the nineteenth century, had one main ambition: to become a successful writer. In fact, it seemed almost predestined that she would strive for that profession. As she herself put it in her introduction to the 1831 edition of *Frankenstein,*

> It is not singular [unusual] that, as the daughter of two persons of distinguished literary celebrity, I should very early in life have thought of writing. As a child I scribbled; and my favorite pastime during the hours given me for recreation was to "write stories."[4]

The parents to whom she referred were William Godwin (1756–1836), an ex-minister turned atheist who became a renowned novelist and essayist, and Mary Wollstonecraft (1759–1797), a pioneering feminist writer. In works such as Godwin's *Enquiry Concerning Political Justice* (1793) and Wollstonecraft's *A Vindication of the Rights of Woman* (1792), the couple, mavericks for their time, strongly advocated the concept of complete personal and intellectual freedom.

Mary Wollstonecraft and William Godwin's daughter, Mary, was born on August 30, 1797, in London. At the time, Wollstonecraft already had a three-year-old daughter, Fanny, who had been born out of wedlock. (Fanny's father was an American merchant named Gilbert Imlay.) Mary Wollstonecraft died from complications of childbirth only a few days after her second daughter's birth. This was the first of a series of tragic losses that Mary Godwin (later Mary Shelley) would endure in her relatively short lifetime.

The untimely death of Mary Wollstonecraft left William Godwin emotionally crushed and faced with raising two young girls on his own. Because he did not feel up to the task and also because he believed Mary and Fanny needed a mother, he married his next-door neighbor, Mary Jane Clairmont, in 1801. The new wife came to the marriage with two children of her own, including young Jane (later called Claire).

From the start, Mary Godwin did not get along with her new stepmother and stepsister Claire. And although the future author of *Frankenstein* dearly loved her father, for the rest of her life she could not help feeling that he had emotionally abandoned her in

Noted feminist and writer Mary Wollstonecraft died soon after giving birth to Mary Godwin in August 1797.

13

favor of his new family. A number of later scholars have suggested that Victor Frankenstein's rejection of the creature, who is in a sense his son, is an expression and projection of the author's own deep-seated feelings. According to Mary's distinguished modern biographer Anne K. Mellor, for example,

> The [creature's] autobiographical account of a benevolent disposition [friendly nature] perverted by social neglect drew most directly on Mary Shelley's own experience of childhood abandonment and emotional deprivation in the Godwin household after her father's remarriage to the unsympathetic Mrs. Clairmont.[5]

A Stream of Intellectual Giants

Whatever her personal feelings, Mary Godwin did remain in awe of her father, who made her constantly aware that she was the daughter of famous and gifted parents. A steady stream of intellectual giants visited the household during her childhood, some of whom she came to know well. These included poet Samuel Taylor Coleridge (author of *The Rime of the Ancient Mariner*, which later became an important thematic source for *Frankenstein*); chemist Sir Humphry Davy (whose world-renowned experiments influenced the use of science in the novel); and writer Charles Lamb (author of the widely read *Tales from Shakespeare*). Hobnobbing with such figures was

William Godwin was unprepared for the arduous task of raising two daughters by himself, so he quickly remarried.

undoubtedly an education in itself. And in fact, Mary did not attend a formal school; instead, Godwin educated her at home. Her tutoring presumably followed the precepts Godwin outlined in an 1802 letter to a friend:

> You enquire respecting the books I think best adapted for the education of female children from the age of two to twelve. I can answer you best on the early part of the subject, because in that I have made the most experiments; and in that part I should make no difference between children male and female. . . . I will put down the names of a few books, calculated to excite the imagination, and at the same time quicken the apprehensions of children. The best I know is a little French book, entitled "Contes de ma Mère, or Tales of Mother Goose." I should also recommend "Beauty and the Beast," "Fortunatus," and a story of a queen and country maid in . . . "Dialogues of the Dead." Your own memory will easily suggest others . . . such as "Valentine and Orson" . . . "Robinson Crusoe" . . . and the "Arabian Nights." I would undoubtedly introduce before twelve years of age some smattering of geography, history, and the other sciences; but it is the train of reading I have here mentioned which I should principally depend upon for generating an active mind and warm heart.[6]

Godwin encouraged his daughter's literary interests so much that in 1808, when she was only eleven, he published a short book of her verses titled *Mounseer Nongtongpaw; or the Discoveries of John Bull in a Trip to Paris.*[7]

Percy Shelley's Pilgrimages

Among the intellectual visitors to the Godwin household, one was to have a far more profound and lasting effect on Mary's life than any other. He was poet Percy Bysshe Shelley, who had been greatly impressed and moved by William Godwin's famous tract on political justice. In 1814, at age nineteen, Percy Shelley began making pilgrimages to Godwin's residence on London's Skinner Street, where the two men engaged fervently in political and literary talk. Mary, who had just returned from an almost two-year stay with family friends in Scotland, was immediately smitten with the handsome, eloquent young poet, and he was equally drawn to her. They began taking long walks together and fell deeply in love. A shadow hung over the relationship, however—namely, the fact that Percy had a young wife named Harriet and two young children by her, whom he now all but abandoned for Mary.

William Godwin was livid when he discovered that his daughter had become attached to a married man. And Per-

Handsome, brilliant, and charming poet Percy Bysshe Shelley became the object of young Mary Godwin's affections.

cy's family was similarly outraged. To escape the uncomfortable atmosphere, in July 1814 Mary and Percy ran off to the "Continent," the common English term for the European mainland. With them went Mary's stepsister, Claire Clairmont, who supposedly wanted to share in what promised to be an exciting and romantic adventure. However, the trip turned out to be far from exciting or romantic for all concerned. The three had little money and found traveling without it difficult and unrewarding. Moreover, Mary despised Claire's presence. "Now, I would not go to Paradise with her as a companion," Mary later wrote. "She poisoned my life when young . . . [and] she has still the faculty of making me more uncomfortable than any human being."[8]

The disenchanted travelers returned to England at the end of the summer. In February of the following year (1815), Mary had her first child, a daughter who died unnamed after a few days. (A few scholars maintain that the baby did receive a name —Clara.) It was a harrowing experience for the seventeen-year-old mother. In March, she had two morbid dreams about the dead child, recording in her journal:

> Dream[ed] that my little baby came to life again; that it had only been cold, and that we rubbed it before the fire, and it lived. Awake[d] and [found] no baby. I think about the little thing all day. Not in good spirits.[9]

This incident may or may not have had any influence on the development of the central concept of *Frankenstein*. If it did not, the association of fire with bringing the dead to life certainly constitutes a bizarre piece of coincidence and foreshadowing.

The Birth of *Frankenstein*

Mary soon became pregnant again, which seemed to lift her gloomy mood somewhat. The apparently healthy child was born in January 1816, and she and Percy named the boy

Lord Byron, the romantic English poet, found that Percy Shelley and Mary Godwin shared his tastes in literature and art, and the three became fast friends.

William after Mary's father. In April, Mary's spirits received a further lift when Claire confided to her and Percy an important secret. The renowned English poet Lord Byron, whom Mary and Percy greatly admired but had never met, had just left England for a rented villa in Switzerland. Shortly before his departure, he and Claire had made love, and supposedly because of his strong feelings for Claire, Byron had invited Mary and Percy to accompany Claire on a forthcoming visit to Switzerland.

As it turned out, Claire's story was only partly true. She had indeed slept with Byron. But he was an infamous ladies' man who had had intimate relations with dozens of women and, finding Claire mundane, had at first rebuffed her advances. To get into his good graces, Claire had promised to introduce him to the daughter of William Godwin, whom Byron held in high regard.

This is how Mary, Percy, their infant son William, and Claire Clairmont ended up in Geneva, Switzerland, in the summer of 1816. Mary and Percy rented a villa only a ten-minute walk from Byron's larger and more elegant Villa Diodati, where the great epic poet John Milton had once stayed. At Villa Diodati one night, Mary, Percy, and Byron engaged in a friendly competition over who could invent the most chilling ghost story. Over the ensuing days, Mary conceived the central characters and concept of what soon developed into a full-fledged novel of gothic horror—*Frankenstein*. Once the work was finished, Percy, a much more experienced writer, offered to help by making minor revisions in grammar and word usage; Mary happily accepted.

Percy Shelley also helped with the book by making arrangements to have an English publisher, Lackington, which had handled some of his own writings, release it. Perhaps because they felt that no publisher would take seriously a work produced by a teenage girl, Mary and Percy decided it would be best to keep the author's identity a secret. The novel was published anonymously in March 1818. Most people assumed

The luxurious and atmospheric Villa Diodati in Geneva, Switzerland, was the scene of the "ghost story" competition that gave birth to Mary Shelley's immortal tale.

that Percy Shelley had created it, partly because it was so well written and also because he provided the preface.

The novel proved to be a best-seller; however, the reviews were decidedly mixed. Some thought it was sensational and trashy, as exemplified by the critic of the *Edinburgh Review:*

> When we have thus admitted that *Frankenstein* has passages that appeal [to] the mind and make the flesh creep, we have given it all the praise (if praise it can be called) which we dare bestow. Our taste and judgment alike revolt at this kind of writing, and the greater the ability with which it may be executed, the worse it is.[10]

Somewhat kinder was the *Edinburgh Magazine*'s review, which stated, "There never was a wilder story imagined; yet, like most fictions of this age, it has an air of reality attached to it by being connected with the favorite [scientific] projects and passions of the times."[11] A few critics even thought the book was exceptionally good. One critic representing *Blackwood's Edinburgh Magazine* (who, like most other people, thought Percy Shelley was the author) declared,

> Upon the whole, the work impresses us with the high idea of the author's original genius and happy power of expression. We shall be delighted to hear that he has aspired to *paullo majora* ["greater things," that is, a work larger and more complex than his customary poems]; and in the meantime, congratulate our readers upon a novel which excites new reflections and untried sources of emotion.[12]

Although the bulk of the novel's literary qualities and social relevance was not fully apparent to most people when it was first published, the story told in *Frankenstein* nonetheless touched a nerve in the public imagination. This is evidenced by the appearance in 1823, only months after the release of the book's second edition and the disclosure that

Mary was the author, of the first of thousands of stage (and later film) adaptations of *Frankenstein*. The play, written by Richard B. Peake, was titled *Presumption: Or, the Fate of Frankenstein*. It starred the then widely popular stage actors James Wallack and Thomas Potter Cooke as Frankenstein and the creature, respectively.

A Series of Crucial Events

Meanwhile, the writing and publication of two editions of *Frankenstein* were certainly not all that occupied Mary Godwin between 1816 and 1823. In late August 1816, Mary, Percy, their young son William, and Claire Clairmont departed the Villa Diodati, where Mary had conceived the germinal elements of *Frankenstein*, and returned to England. During the next several months, as Mary labored on what would prove to be her greatest literary work, she and Percy were repeatedly distracted by crucial events, most of them tragic or unfortunate.

Percy Shelley writes one of his masterpieces in a painting by Joseph Severn. Because Shelley wrote the preface to Frankenstein, *most critics assumed he had written the novel.*

First, in October, Fanny Godwin, Mary's half-sister, committed suicide (and was buried anonymously because her father refused to identify or claim the body). Then, in December, the body of Percy Shelley's wife, Harriet, turned up in a river. She too had taken her own life. Apparently, the combination of the embarrassment over her husband's abandoning her, the strain of raising their two young children on her own, and the fact that she had recently become pregnant by another man was too much for her to bear.

Mary and Percy now found themselves contemplating marriage. They had long viewed entering this traditional and formal social union as unnecessary. But Harriet's family was threatening to keep Percy Shelley from getting custody of the children and his lawyers suggested that wedding Mary might make him look more respectable in the eyes of the courts. The ceremony took place on December 30, 1816, at St. Mildred's Church in London. Mary Godwin now officially became Mary Shelley. Her father, who had remained distant for some two years, was relieved and delighted. "According to the vulgar ideas of the world, she is well married," Godwin wrote to his brother,

> and I have great hopes the young man will make her a good husband. You will wonder, I dare say, how a girl without a penny of fortune should meet with so good a match. But such are the ups and downs of this world.[13]

But while the marriage pleased Godwin, it did not move the courts. In March 1817 Percy Shelley lost custody of his and Harriet's children, and the evidence suggests that he never saw them again.

Plagued by Tragedies

For Mary Shelley, the next few years provided ample confirmation of the "ups and downs of this world" of which her father had spoken. On the positive side, she traveled to the

Continent, spending many pleasant months in Italy. And after *Frankenstein*'s first publication early in 1818, she worked fairly steadily on two more novels, *Valperga* and *Mathilda*.

On the negative side, these same years were plagued by intermittent tragedies. In September 1817, Mary gave birth to a daughter, whom she and Percy named Clara Everina, but the baby died of fever just over a year later. Then, in June 1819, when Mary was twenty-one, William, then three, died of malaria (or possibly cholera). Mary, who was already pregnant for a fourth time, suffered from deep depression for some time afterward. Her mood improved markedly after the new baby, Percy Florence, was born in November of that year. He would be the only one of Mary's children to survive into adulthood.

All of the tragedies Mary had endured so far in her life paled in significance, however, to that which struck in July 1822. Percy Shelley and a friend, Edward Williams, went sailing off the western Italian coast in Shelley's small boat, the *Don Juan*.

Percy Shelley's body is cremated on an Italian beach on July 19, 1822, after his accidental drowning. Crushed by the loss of her soul mate, Mary Shelley never fully recovered.

23

An unexpected storm suddenly descended on the area, the boat disappeared, and for ten days teams of searchers combed the coastal beaches and inlets. On July 19, Mary was finally informed that the drowned bodies of the two men had been found washed up on a beach. Stoically, undoubtedly in a state of shock, Mary visited the beach the next morning and viewed the three white sticks that marked her husband's temporary grave. "I never saw such a scene—nor wish to see such another,"[14] was how Byron described Mary's mental and emotional state when he visited her a few weeks later.

In all likelihood, it was Mary's youth and resilience that allowed her to muster the strength to survive the loss of her husband. One way she found of coping was to deify him and his memory in the true and resplendent manner of the poets and other artists of her highly romantic era. That process began almost immediately, as evidenced by this passage from a letter she wrote to a friend later in 1822:

> I was fortunate in having [been] fearlessly placed by destiny in the hands of one, who was a superior being among men, a bright planetary spirit enshrined in an earthly temple, raised me to the height of happiness— so far am I now happy that I would not change my situation as His widow with that of the most prosperous woman in the world—and surely the time will at length come when I shall be at peace & my brain & heart be no longer alive with unutterable anguish. I can conceive but of one circumstance that could afford me the semblance of content—that is the being permitted to live where I am now in the same house, in the same state, occupied alone with my child, in collecting His manuscripts—writing his life, and thus to go easily to my grave.[15]

Mary's efforts to glorify Percy Shelley's memory continued. The following two years witnessed her collection, editing, and publication of his previously unpublished poems in a volume titled *Posthumous Poems of Percy Bysshe Shelley.* But admirable as these and other such efforts were, they took their toll on a young woman who, if she had not been so haunted by the dead, still might have found a happy, fulfilled life. "She overcompensated by recreating Percy Shelley in the image of a living god," says Anne Mellor.

> And in so doing, she both denigrated [downplayed and belittled] herself and rendered it impossible to establish normal, healthy relationships with other men. Always the shadow of Percy Shelley came between them.[16]

This was surely the reason that Mary refused two proposals of marriage. The first was in 1825 from John Howard Payne, an American actor-manager, and the second in 1831 from Edward Trelawny, a friend she and Percy had known in Italy.

Her First Novel Still Her Best

In a very real way, the phantom of Percy Shelley continued to haunt Mary the rest of her days. Some of her most important later writings contain tributes to him, often in the guise of characters that are clearly modeled on him. The novel *The Last Man,* published in 1826, for instance, features two characters, Adrian, earl of

American actor John Howard Payne was one of the men who proposed marriage to Mary in her later years. Mary declined, haunted by Percy Shelley's memory.

Windsor, and Lord Raymond, who are much like Percy Shelley and Lord Byron (who died of fever, at age thirty-six, in Greece in April 1824).

It must be pointed out that neither *The Last Man* nor any of Mary's other novels ever matched the literary quality or public popularity of *Frankenstein*. Her inability to turn out another masterpiece in her more mature years may have been partly the result of the emotional roller coaster that her long series of tragedies forced her to ride. Some scholars suggest that it was the very fact that when she conceived *Frankenstein*

The most famous portrait of Mary Shelley was painted in 1841 by noted artist Richard Rothwell. It captures her high forehead, refined features, and keen intelligence.

she was so young, full of exuberance, and not yet encumbered by heavy worries and responsibilities that gave the novel its power. In the view of biographer Muriel Spark,

> *Frankenstein* is Mary Shelley's best novel because at that age she was not yet well acquainted with her own mind. As her self-insight grew—and she was exceptionally introspective [absorbed in self-examination]—so did her work suffer from causes the very opposite of her intention; and what very often mars her later writing is its extreme explicitness [its detailed descriptions, leaving little to the imagination]. In *Frankenstein,* however, it is the implicit utterance [unstated ideas lurking beneath the narrative's surface] which gives the theme its power.[17]

For the rest of her life, Mary Shelley knew well that the tale of Victor Frankenstein and his monstrous creation was her most successful work. She may also have sensed that it was the best, for she labored diligently at refurbishing and rewriting it for the release of its third edition in 1831. It was for this edition that she penned the now famous and often-quoted introduction explaining how she had conceived of the characters and ideas. "The publishers," she began,

> in selecting *Frankenstein* for one of their series, expressed a wish that I should furnish them with some account of the origin of the story. I am the more willing to comply, because I shall thus give a general answer to the question, so very frequently asked me —"How I, then a young girl, came to think of and to dilate upon so very hideous an idea?"[18]

She then gave a detailed recollection of her stay at the Villa Diodati, the ghost story contest with Percy and Byron, and how the principal concepts came to her at night in her darkened bedroom.

After the reissue of the novel, Mary lived long enough to see her son, Percy Florence, the only surviving relative or friend from her early life, grow up and get married in 1848. Then, following a series of strokes, she died in London on February 1, 1851, at the age of fifty-three. Her son saw that she was buried between the remains of her mother and father, whose creative talents she had inherited.

Less than two years before, the fourth stage version of her most famous novel, a musical comedy titled *Frankenstein: Or, the Vampire's Victim,* had opened in London. No one at the time could have foreseen that this was only the initial trickle of a veritable flood of flamboyant adaptations of the work that would appear in the ensuing century and a half. Certainly, Mary Shelley would have been surprised to find that the novel and its literary and film offspring would make her name immortal.

The Sources of the Ideas for *Frankenstein*

ccording to its author, the main characters and central concept of *Frankenstein* were first conceived in a darkened room with "closed shutters, with moonlight struggling through," and a "glassy lake and white high Alps beyond."[19] The room was Mary Shelley's bedchamber in Lord Byron's majestic and highly romantic Villa Diodati, nestled along the shores of Lake Geneva in Switzerland. The year was 1816, and, as Mary later recalled, it had been a "wet, ungenial [unfriendly] summer, and incessant rain often confined us for days to the house."[20] To while away the time, Byron and his guests —Mary, Percy Shelley, and

Lord Byron sits on the veranda of Villa Diodati. It was in this imposing mansion that the idea for Frankenstein *came to Mary Shelley.*

Shelley focused on the idea of humans playing God by creating life. This became the central core of her novel and the many films based on it, including Son of Frankenstein *(1939), depicted here.*

Byron's handsome young doctor and friend, John Polidori—engaged in discussions of literature, as well as various intellectual and often controversial topics.

One night, not long after acquiring some German ghost stories that had been translated into French, Byron suddenly exclaimed, "We will each write a ghost story!" According to Mary's later recollection,

> There were four of us. The noble author [Byron] began a tale, a fragment of which he [later] printed at the end of his poem *Mazeppa* [published in 1819]. [Percy] Shelley, more apt to embody ideas and senti-

ments in the radiance of brilliant imagery . . . commenced one founded on the experiences of his early life. Poor Polidori had some terrible idea about a skull-headed lady who was . . . punished for peeping through a keyhole. . . . I busied myself *to think of a story* . . . one which would speak to the mysterious fears of our nature and awaken thrilling horror—one to make the reader dread to look round, to curdle the blood and quicken the beatings of the heart. If I did not accomplish these things, my ghost story would be unworthy of its name.[21]

For several days, Mary was unable to come up with just the right story. In the meantime, more intellectual conversations ensued. Byron and Percy discussed the nature and principle of life, the latest scientific discoveries, and whether such discoveries might allow a human to usurp God's role and create life. An eerie, almost spooky mood having been created, that night Mary retired to her room, the one with the "closed shutters with moonlight struggling through." Unable to sleep, all at once she was inundated by a flood of stark and disturbing ideas and images. "My imagination, unbidden, possessed and guided me," she wrote later,

gifting the successive images that arose in my mind with a vividness far beyond the usual bounds of reverie [daydreaming]. I saw—with shut eyes, but acute mental vision—I saw the pale student of unhallowed [unholy] arts kneeling beside the thing he had put together. I saw the hideous phantasm of a man stretched out, and then, on the working of some powerful engine [machine], show signs of life, and stir with an uneasy, half-vital motion. Frightful must it be; for supremely frightful would be the effect of any human endeavor to mock the stupendous mechanism [plan] of the Creator of the world. His success would terrify the artist [inventor]. . . . He might sleep in the belief that the silence of the grave would quench forever the transient [passing] existence of the hideous corpse which he had looked upon as the cradle of life. He sleeps; but he is awakened. He opens his eyes; behold the horrid thing [that he has created] stands at his bedside, opening his curtains, and looking on him with yellow, watery, but speculative [questioning] eyes. I opened mine in terror. The idea so possessed my mind, that a thrill of fear ran through me.[22]

Develop the Idea at Greater Length?

Victor Frankenstein and his monstrous creature had been born. Their teenage creator could not wait to tell Percy and the others, and early the next morning she "announced" to them "that I had *thought of a story.*"[23] So far, all she had were the bare bones—basically the notion of a human researcher who successfully endows a corpse with life. To expand this idea into a short story, or perhaps even a novel, Mary would need to conceive of other appropriate concepts and themes and develop them. She later recalled how the work subsequently began to take shape:

> At first I thought but a few pages—of a short tale; but Shelley urged me to develop the idea at greater length. I certainly did not owe the suggestion of one incident, nor scarcely of one train of feeling to my husband, and yet but for his incitement it would never have taken the form in which it [the tale] was presented to the world. From this declaration I must except the preface. As far as I can recollect, it was entirely written by him.[24]

Percy Shelley did indeed write the preface to the novel. It is written in the first person, giving the surface impression that the person who wrote it wrote the novel as well. For instance, one passage reads:

The circumstance on which my story rests was suggested in casual conversation. It was commenced partly as a source of amusement, and partly as an expedient [resource] for exercising any untried resources of mind. Other motives were mingled with these as the work proceeded. I am by no means indifferent to the manner in which whatever moral tendencies exist in the sentiments or characters it contains shall affect the reader; yet my chief concern in this respect has been limited to avoiding the . . . effects of the novels of the present day.[25]

With the intention of helping a young, inexperienced writer, Shelley also made several stylistic modifications to the text. In various places, for example, he changed "talked" to "conversed," "felt" to "endured," "hot" to "inflamed," "die" to "perish," and "ghost-story" to "a tale of superstition." Typical of some of his changes in longer phrases was his substitution of "a considerable time period elapsed" for Mary's "it was a long time," and his "in compliance with his favorite theory, that learning was superfluous in the commerce of ordinary life" for her "said he did not see of what use learning could be to a merchant."[26]

Gladly accepting Shelley's preface and minor modifications, Mary finished the novel in May 1817. Byron read the manuscript.

Percy Shelley, painted by artist Amelia Curran in 1819, made a number of small but significant modifications to the original text of Frankenstein.

And in a letter to a friend, he gave this assessment: "Methinks it is a wonderful work for a girl of nineteen."[27]

The Use and Misuse of Science

Later generations of critics and readers have heartily concurred with Byron. They have also praised the novel's originality, ingenuity of conception and execution, and discerning foreshadowing of some of the most significant scientific challenges and problems of modern technological civilization. Indeed, some of the scientific principles emerging in Mary

English chemist Humphry Davy, shown in a portrait by Thomas Lawrence, performed experiments in which he used electricity to make the muscles of dead animals twitch.

Shelley's day, as well as the potential misuse of these discoveries, were among the chief sources of her ideas for the story.

For example, in the years directly preceding Mary's writing of *Frankenstein,* scientists had begun to make huge strides toward understanding the workings of nature. Among those researchers whose works she read and who inspired her was English chemist Sir Humphry Davy (1778–1829). He experimented with galvanism, the application of electrical currents to animal tissues. Electricity, Davy demonstrated, could make the muscles of dismembered legs from frogs and other animals twitch and move almost as they had when the creatures were alive. He and some other scientists suggested that electricity might be a crucial component of living tissues.

Impressed with this idea, Mary Shelley utilized it in her novel. Though she never describes in detail the process by which Victor Frankenstein animates the creature, she makes several references in the story to lightning and electricity as special, elemental forces connected somehow with life. "I was not unacquainted with the more obvious laws of electricity," Frankenstein says in the early part of his narrative. Then a noted researcher "entered on an explanation of the theory which he had formed on the subject of electricity and galvanism, which was at once new and astonishing to me."[28] And later, having assembled the creature, Frankenstein recalls, "I collected the instruments of life around me, that I might infuse a spark of being into the lifeless thing that lay at my feet."[29]

Another scientific source Mary drew on for the novel was English biologist Erasmus Darwin (1731–1802), whom she had met as a child when he had paid visits to her father. She remembered hearing Shelley and Byron discussing "the experiments of Dr. Darwin . . . who preserved a piece of vermicelli [a kind of pasta] in a glass case, till by some means it began to move with voluntary motion."[30] Darwin was a distinguished researcher who dabbled in many areas of science and introduced a theory of evolution that foreshadowed the more comprehensive and famous one later formulated by his grandson, Charles Darwin. Mary's reference to Erasmus Darwin's "moving vermicelli" was a distorted memory of Darwin's written description of "animalcules," or microscopic creatures, growing in a mixture of flour and water. The scientist speculated that this and other forms of life might appear spontaneously under certain conditions. In Mary's mind, this idea strengthened the believability that Victor Frankenstein, a young and inexperienced researcher, could stumble on important secrets of life.

As penned by Mary Shelley, Victor Frankenstein also makes the mistake of trying to find a shortcut to evolution, the long natural process of creating new species that Erasmus Darwin had described. According to Anne Mellor,

> Reading *Frankenstein* in the context of Darwin's writings, we can see that Mary Shelley directly pitted Victor Frankenstein . . . against those gradual evolutionary processes of nature so well described by Darwin. Rather than letting organic life-forms evolve slowly over thousands of years according to natural processes of sexual selection, Victor Frankenstein wants to organize a new life-form quickly, by chemical means. . . . Significantly, in his attempt to create a new species, [he] substitutes [creation by a single father figure] for sexual reproduction. He thus reverses the evolutionary ladder described by Darwin. And he engages in a concept of science that Mary Shelley deplores, the notion that science should manipulate and control rather than describe, understand, and revere nature.[31]

Indeed, this potential for the misuse of science seemed to haunt Mary. She was never in much doubt that the forward march of science would one day reveal the secrets of life and death. For her, as well as for the insightful Shelley and Byron, the more important question was whether scientists would

Kenneth Branagh portrays Victor Frankenstein as he toils desperately to create life through chemical means in the 1994 film Mary Shelley's Frankenstein.

use their discoveries wisely and beneficially. The core ideas of their frequent discussions of this topic eventually found their way into the novel. In this way, Mary Shelley became one of the first modern thinkers to foresee that science, though having the potential to greatly benefit humanity, might also inadvertently unleash destructive forces. Her novel developed this theme so well that the phrase "to create a Frankenstein" has become a universally recognized description of science's unexpected and unwanted by-products.

The Myths of Prometheus

Science was only one of the sources for the ideas Mary Shelley developed in *Frankenstein*. She also drew and expanded on some important literary works and themes. Chief among these were the ancient Greek myths of Prometheus, from which the book's subtitle, *The Modern Prometheus,* derived. One of an early race of Greek gods known as the Titans, Prometheus and the tales of his exploits had long fascinated Mary, Byron, and Shelley. (Both Byron and Shelley composed works based on the Prometheus myths.)

One of these ancient tales told of Prometheus *plastictor,* or molder, who fashioned humans from clay; the other told of Prometheus *pyrphoros,* or fire wielder, who gave knowledge of fire to humans. In the original myths, Prometheus, whose name meant "forethought," was the son of the Titans Iapetus and Themis. There was a great war in the heavens between the Titans and a younger race of gods, the Olympians, led by Zeus. After the Olympians won, Zeus noted with pleasure that Prometheus had fought on the Olympians' side, so the leader of the gods did not condemn Prometheus to eternal captivity in the Underworld, as he did most of the other Titans.

A giant bird gnaws at the liver of the chained god Prometheus. The Prometheus myths were a major inspiration for Mary Shelley's great novel.

Not long after the war's conclusion, Prometheus decided to fashion the first humans out of clay. The goddess Athena then breathed life into them. Later, Zeus asked the Titan to decide how the humans should go about making sacrifices to the gods. Partial to his creations, the wily Prometheus tricked Zeus by arranging for the gods to receive the bones and fat of the animals sacrificed and for the humans to keep and eat the meat. In retaliation, Zeus denied the humans knowledge of fire.

Seeing that the tiny beings he had created lacked fire to cook meat and fashion tools, Prometheus felt great pity for them. Soon he daringly defied Zeus by stealing some fire from heaven and giving it to the humans. The angry Zeus then punished the Titan by having Hephaestos (god of the forge) chain him to a mountaintop, where a giant vulture daily devoured his liver, which grew back at night.

The Spark of Divine Fire

Over time, as the myths were told and retold over successive generations, Prometheus's two main deeds—creating humans and stealing divine fire—merged into one. Prometheus usurped Athena's role in the original myths, and most people came to envision him using the stolen heavenly fire to bring his human figures to life. "This gave a radically new significance to the myth," points out M.K. Joseph, a former professor at the University of Auckland in New Zealand. Prometheus became a sort of "deputy creator," a concept

> which could also be readily allegorized [made into a story that illustrates or symbolizes some aspect of human existence] by the Christians and was frequently used in the Middle Ages as a representation of the creative power of God. By the Renaissance, the image was a familiar one. . . . Later still, Prometheus became an accepted image of the creative artist.[32]

Mary Shelley grew up with this image of creative individuals embodying the age-old spirit of Prometheus. And she effectively wove both Promethean roles—molder of life and fire giver—into the fabric of her novel *Frankenstein,* suggesting that Victor Frankenstein is a modern Prometheus. On

Prometheus snatches a bit of fire from heaven to give to his beloved creations —human beings. As depicted in the novel, Victor Frankenstein is the "modern Prometheus."

the one hand, he shapes a human body from various spare body parts and other materials; on the other, he infuses his nonliving creation with a spark of electricity, a kind of divine fire. In this way, Mary created a link between the Promethean myths and the then-current scientific ideas about the possibilities of electricity acting as a vital spark of life.

Today, after quantum leaps of scientific progress and seemingly endless literary and filmic spin-offs of the Frankenstein story, few people recognize just how radical and revolutionary this use of the Prometheus legends was at the time. All educated people in Mary Shelley's day recognized Prometheus as a metaphor for the creative artist. But people then did not generally think of scientists as artists or creators; rather, they were seen as searchers of knowledge and experimenters seeking new ways to use known materials. The idea of a scientist creating life in the manner of Prometheus had momentous consequences. Chief among these was the arrogance of a human usurping the duties normally reserved for God. At the time, such a notion was at the least shocking and disturbing and in the eyes of some even blasphemous and immoral. In Mary's new and controversial twist, Joseph explains,

> the scientist, himself a creature, has taken on the role and burden of a creator. If Frankenstein corrupts the monster by his rejection . . . we are left asking a question which demands another kind of answer. What has rejected and corrupted Frankenstein? [God, perhaps?] And if Prometheus . . . is identified with human revolt, is the monster what that revolt looks like from the other side—a pitiful botched-up creature, a "filthy mass that moved and talked," which brings nothing but grief and destruction upon the power that made him? . . . At the age of nineteen, [Mary Shelley] achieved the quietly astonishing feat of . . . creating a lasting symbol of the perils of scientific Prometheanism.[33]

Adam and Satan Converge

Another of Mary Shelley's important literary sources for the central concepts of *Frankenstein* also deals with a higher being infusing nonliving materials with life; in this case, it is God's creation of the first human, Adam, in the Judeo-Christian Bible. But in exploiting Adam's story, Mary relied less on the original source and more on a renowned literary work based on the biblical account. In 1667, English poet John Milton (1608–1674) published the epic poem *Paradise Lost*. Its sweeping verses tell the timeless tale of how Satan got Adam and Eve to commit the first sin, a transgression for which God expelled them from the Garden of Eden. It also describes how in an earlier age Satan had been an angel who rebelled against God and was expelled from heaven.

In writing *Frankenstein*, Mary Shelley recognized that the creature Victor Frankenstein creates has much in common with Milton's Adam. Each is an innocent being who wakes up in a strange world that he (or it) does not understand and must learn to survive and cope in that world by trial and error. Thus, it is no accident that, in the novel, much of the creature's self-education is based on reading a copy of Milton's *Paradise Lost* that it finds discarded in the forest. The creature immediately recognizes in Adam's situation and predicaments some similarities to its own; however, it also sadly sees many dissimilarities. "Like Adam," the creature tells Victor Frankenstein,

> I was apparently united by no link to any other being in existence; but his state was far different than mine. . . . He had come forth from the hands of God a perfect creature, happy and prosperous, guarded by the especial care of his Creator; he was allowed to converse with, and acquire knowledge from, beings of a superior nature. But I was wretched, helpless, and alone. Many times I considered Satan as the fitter em-

Michelangelo's The Creation of Adam *shows God infusing Adam with life. In Mary Shelley's novel, the creature sees itself more like Satan than Adam.*

blem of my condition; for often, like him, when I viewed the bliss of my protectors, the bitter gall of envy rose within me. . . . No Eve soothed my sorrows, nor shared my thoughts; I was alone. I remembered Adam's supplication to his Creator. But where was mine? He had abandoned me; and, in the bitterness of my heart, I cursed him.[34]

The creature's remark that it sometimes identifies itself more with Satan than with Adam is telling. In the course of the story, the wretched being evolves from an innocent, confused, lonely Adam-like figure into a vengeful, destructive, pitiless Satan-like figure. As Milton shows in *Paradise Lost*, Satan had begun as an angel and then fell from grace. So too does the creature feel its benevolent qualities steadily slipping away as its Adam-like and Satan-like traits converge. Milton's Satan is a fascinating character, yet Mary Shelley creates a character even more compelling by making the creature more pitiful and pathetic than Satan. The creature "is worse off than Satan," Christopher Small points out. At least Satan

Satan, with whom the creature relates, began as an angel (pictured here) but later fell from grace. The creature regrets that, unlike Satan, it began its existence without ever knowing grace.

started out belonging to the heavenly host and later has the support of the residents of hell; Frankenstein's creation is

> exiled from the start. . . . [It] belongs nowhere and to nobody. As the story progresses, so [it] becomes progressively more Satanic, [its] powers growing to positively fiendish capacity (it is alluded to more often as "the fiend" in the later part of the book) and its ill deeds multiplying accordingly. . . . In [its] second confrontation with Frankenstein . . . [it] addresses him as "slave"—"you are my creator, but I am your master," and threatens him: "Beware; for I am fearless, and therefore powerful." . . . Not surprisingly, Frankenstein in reply calls [it] simply "devil."[35]

Later, the formerly Adam-like creature completes its transformation into a Satan-like creature. Like Satan in *Paradise Lost,* the creature remembers its lost innocence but finds it hard to believe that it once strove to be good and decent and to live in harmony with humans. It declares:

> I cannot believe that I am the same creature whose thoughts were once filled with sublime [grand] and transcendent visions of the beauty and majesty of goodness. But it is even so. The fallen angel becomes a malignant [evil] devil. Yet even that enemy of God and man [Satan] had friends and associates in his desolation; I am alone.[36]

As a literary source of ideas for Mary Shelley's novel, therefore, Milton's masterpiece is no less crucial than the myths of Prometheus. Mary's ability to build major elements of character, plot, and theme around the concepts of these sources is a testament to her skill, her good taste, and above all her imagination. *Frankenstein* remains one of the most stunning examples in literature of creating a new, daring, and revolutionary twist on old ideas.

CHAPTER THREE

The Story Told in *Frankenstein*

The narrative Mary Shelley lays out in her most famous novel is told in flashback. Most of the time it is a double flashback, a sort of story within a story, and at one point a third story is told within the second. All three stories are told in the first person, giving them a strong feeling of immediacy and authenticity.

The first story opens with four brief letters written by a ship captain and explorer named Robert Walton to his sister Margaret. Walton explains that he and his crew are making their way through the Arctic wastes near the North Pole, hoping to find a navigable water route to the northern Pacific Ocean. Walton also tells his sister that he is lonely and desires a true friend with whom he can share his inner thoughts and excitement about his work. "When I am glowing with the enthusiasm of success," he writes,

> there will be none to participate [in] my joy. . . . I shall commit my thoughts to paper it is true; but that is a poor medium for the communication of feeling. I de-

sire the company of a man who could sympathize with me; whose eyes would reply to mine. You may deem me romantic, my dear sister, but I bitterly feel the want [lack] of a friend.[37]

One day while moving slowly through a vast ice-choked channel, Walton tells Margaret, he and his men saw an exceptionally strange sight. "We perceived a low carriage, fixed on a sledge [a strong, heavy sled] and drawn by dogs . . . at a distance of half a mile." Even more unusual was the fact that the driver was of "gigantic stature." Fascinated, the explorers "watched the rapid progress of the traveler with our telescopes, until he was lost among the distant inequalities of the ice."[38]

The next morning brought another surprise. Near the ship drifted a small chunk of ice on which lay another sledge. This one was carrying a European-looking man who was

Aidan Quinn portrays Captain Robert Walton in Kenneth Branagh's 1994 film. In the opening Walton expresses his loneliness and his desire for a true friend.

clearly in sad shape. "His limbs were nearly frozen," Walton recalls, "and his body dreadfully emaciated by fatigue and suffering. I never saw a man in so wretched a condition."[39] Once the stranger had recovered somewhat, he revealed that his name was Victor Frankenstein and that he had recently been in hot pursuit of the giant figure the explorers had seen traveling across the ice floes.

The days passed by. As Frankenstein's strength returned and he and Walton conversed, Walton believed that he may have finally found the cultured and sympathetic friend he had long sought. Eventually, Frankenstein felt confident enough to tell his story to Walton, who took notes and included them in his latest letter to his sister. Thus begins the second story, Victor Frankenstein's tale, as told within the context of Robert Walton's own narrative.

Victor Frankenstein's Youth

Frankenstein explained that he was born in Geneva, Switzerland, where his father had been a respected leader in local government. When Victor was a boy, the family took a vacation to Italy. There, by chance, they encountered a poor family with five starving children. One, a fair-haired, blue-eyed girl, seemed quite different from the rest, who were all dark-haired. The parents told the Frankensteins that the girl, whose name was Elizabeth, had been left in their care by a nobleman who had since died. Taking pity on the child, Victor's parents adopted her. And soon the boy became strongly attached to his new sibling. "[I] looked upon Elizabeth as mine," Frankenstein recalled,

> mine to protect, love, and cherish. . . . We called each other familiarly by the name of cousin. No word, no expression could body forth the kind of relation in which she stood to me—my more than sister, since to death she was to be mine only.[40]

Not long afterward, the Frankensteins had two more sons of their own—William and Ernest. And the family long enjoyed a happy existence.

The first note of tragedy to mar that existence came when Victor Frankenstein was seventeen. The day before he was scheduled to leave home to begin attending a renowned college in the nearby town of Ingolstadt (on the Danube River in Germany), his mother died of a severe fever. Her last wish was that Victor and Elizabeth would marry and live happily together. After mourning his mother, young Frankenstein departed for Ingolstadt and began his studies.

When Victor Frankenstein's mother (actress Cherie Lunghi) died, her last wish was that he would marry Elizabeth.

The Deepest Mysteries of Creation

Those studies were almost entirely dominated by science classes. All through his youth, Frankenstein had been fascinated, indeed almost obsessed, with trying to understand the secrets of life and death. Ancient alchemists, he had heard, had discovered a mysterious elixir that extended or perhaps even created life. Why could modern researchers not rediscover such lost secrets? At Ingolstadt, a science teacher, Professor Krempe, discouraged the young man from such pursuits. "Have you really spent your time in studying such nonsense?"[41] Krempe asked. By contrast, another of Frankenstein's teachers, Professor Waldman, suggested that ancient knowledge of the secrets of life did exist and might be resurrected.

This filled young Frankenstein with hope and enthusiasm. "Soon my mind was filled with one thought, one conception, one purpose," he remembered.

> So much has been done . . . [but] more, far more will I achieve. Treading in the steps already marked [by earlier researchers], I will pioneer a new way, explore unknown powers, and unfold to the world the deepest mysteries of creation.[42]

Outside of his classes, Frankenstein worked to fulfill his strange quest almost night and day, and it consumed him to such a degree that he began to neglect everything else, including his family. His letters to his father and Elizabeth diminished in number and finally ceased. And he grew thin and pale from a lack of proper meals and rest.

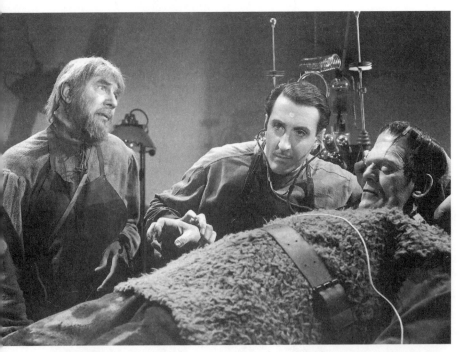

At college, Victor Frankenstein discovered ancient knowledge of the secrets of life. In this scene from Son of Frankenstein, *his son puts that knowledge to use.*

After two years of study and relentless experimentation, the young man finally felt that he was ready to attempt the creation of life. He collected limbs, organs, and other body parts from graves, mortuaries, and other resting places of the dead; with them, he constructed a new human frame some eight feet long. When the gruesome labor was finished, all that was left was for Frankenstein to animate the corpse using the secrets he had recently learned. He recalled with a touch of horror and trembling:

> It was on a dreary night in November, that I beheld the accomplishment of my toils. With an anxiety that almost amounted to agony, I collected the instruments of life around me, that I might infuse a spark of being into the lifeless thing that lay at my feet. It was already one in the morning; the rain pattered dismally against the panes, and my candle was nearly burned out, when, by the glimmer of the half-extinguished light, I saw the dull yellow eye of the creature open; it breathed hard, and a convulsive motion agitated its limbs. . . . Great God! His yellow skin scarcely covered the work of muscles and arteries beneath; his hair was of a lustrous black, and flowing; his teeth of a pearly whiteness; but these [traits] only formed a more horrid contrast with his watery eyes . . . his shriveled complexion, and straight black lips.[43]

The Cycle of Murder Begins

At this seeming moment of triumph, Victor Frankenstein suddenly found himself filled with horror and fear at the hideous thing he had created. The man fled to his bedroom. He was so exhausted from his long days without sleep that he dozed off. He dreamed that he was embracing his beloved Elizabeth, only to see her turn into a rotting corpse with worms crawling out of her. Waking with a start and dripping

After Victor suffered a breakdown, his friend Henry Clerval (played by Tom Hulce) nursed him back to health.

with sweat, the shaken man beheld an even more frightening apparition—the misshapen creature standing over him and mumbling some inarticulate sounds.

Terrified, Frankenstein rushed outside and ran almost aimlessly through the streets until he encountered his good friend Henry Clerval, who had just arrived in Ingolstadt to begin his own studies at the college. The two men rushed back to Frankenstein's lodgings, but the creature was gone. Relieved, the young scientist collapsed and fell into a fever. Luckily for him, over the course of the next few months Henry nursed him back to health and took him on a trip to the countryside to improve his strength and spirits.

When the two men returned to Ingolstadt, a disturbing letter from Frankenstein's father was waiting. Victor's brother William had recently been strangled to death and a hunt for the killer was in progress. Returning to Geneva, the grieving young Victor Frankenstein left the house one night and went to the spot where the murder had occurred. There, as a thunderstorm raged, he had a blood-chilling experience. He recalled:

> This noble war in the sky [the storm] elevated my spirits. I clasped my hands and exclaimed aloud: "William, dear angel! this is your funeral!" . . . As I said these words, I perceived in the gloom a figure which stole from behind a clump of trees near me. . . . A flash of light illuminated the object, and discovered its shape plainly to me; its gigantic stature, and the deformity of

its aspect, more hideous than belongs to humanity, instantly informed me that it was the wretch, the filthy demon to whom I had given life. . . . Could he be . . . the murderer of my brother? No sooner did that idea cross my imagination, than I became convinced of its truth.[44]

The giant figure disappeared into the darkness. Not long afterward, the police arrested Justine Moritz, a servant to the Frankenstein family and a close friend of Elizabeth's, for

A flash of lightning revealed to Victor a shape of "gigantic stature" (portrayed by Robert De Niro in the 1994 film); he instinctively knew it was his creation.

William's murder. Both Frankenstein and Elizabeth were certain of Justine's innocence, Frankenstein especially because he knew the creature was the guilty party. But at the trial, Frankenstein failed to reveal this knowledge for fear of being thought insane. Justine was convicted and executed, leaving the young man more guilty and distraught than ever.

The Creature's Story

After Justine's death, Victor Frankenstein left Geneva and journeyed to towering Mt. Blanc, in the Alps, hoping that a period of solitary hiking and climbing would clear his mind and raise his spirits. But he soon found that he was not alone.

> I suddenly beheld the figure of a man, at some distance, advancing towards me with superhuman speed. . . . His stature, also, as he approached seemed to exceed that of a man. . . . It was the wretch whom I had created. I trembled with rage and horror, resolving to . . . close with him in mortal combat.[45]

However, it quickly became clear that the creature had come to talk, not to fight. Frankenstein hurled obscenities at it, to which it replied: "I expected this reception. All men hate the wretched; how, then, must I be hated, who am miserable beyond all living things!"[46] The creature implored its maker to have pity on it and attempt to understand its plight. "Listen to me, Frankenstein," it said.

> You accuse me of murder; and yet you would, with a satisfied conscience, destroy your own creature. Oh, praise the eternal justice of man! Yet I ask you not to spare me; listen to me; and then, if you can, and if you will, destroy the work of your hands.[47]

Reluctantly, the man listened to the creature's tale, which constitutes the novel's third story, encompassed within Frankenstein's own story. The creature explained how, in the days following its awakening in Frankenstein's lodgings, it was bewildered by its surroundings. It wandered haphazardly through the countryside, searching for any meager food and shelter it might find. Eventually it came to a village, where it sought refuge. But repulsed by the creature's great size and ugliness, the inhabitants reacted with fear and violence. Some of them "attacked me," it recalled, "until, grievously bruised by stones and many other kinds of missile weapons, I escaped to the open country."[48]

In time, the wretch found a miserable wooden shack with an earthen floor, a hovel that adjoined a small but well-kept cottage. Afraid to show itself, the creature began secretly

The creature (Robert De Niro) discovers a wooden shack attached to the cottage of the De Lacey family, whose members it begins to observe.

watching the family that lived in the cottage—the De Laceys, consisting of a father, who was blind; a son, Felix; and a daughter, Agatha. By listening to their conversations and watching their actions, the observer began to learn human language and manners. Then, after many months, Felix brought home a young Turkish girl, Safie, whom the De Laceys adopted. As Felix taught her to speak his own language, the creature, still listening intently from its hiding place, completely mastered the same tongue. It also learned to read after finding three books discarded in the forest—Plutarch's *Parallel Lives*, Milton's *Paradise Lost*, and Goethe's *Sorrows of Young Werther.*

After watching the De Lacey family for a year, the creature decided to approach and offer friendship to the blind father,

In the 1993 TV version of Frankenstein, *the blind Mr. De Lacey (John Mills) receives an offer of friendship from the creature (Randy Quaid), who wants the family to understand its plight.*

who had shown himself to be a kind man. But no sooner had it entered the cottage and greeted the old man when Felix arrived; thinking the monstrous stranger was about to hurt his father, the son drove the intruder from the house.

The creature had earlier found Frankenstein's journal in the coat it had taken when it had departed Ingolstadt. And now that it had been rejected by those it had sought to befriend, it endeavored to seek out its creator for companionship. Arriving in Geneva after a difficult journey, the wretch came upon a young boy playing near the Frankenstein house. It made friendly overtures to the lad, but in vain. The boy, who turned out to be Victor's brother William, called it a "hideous monster," a "wretch," and an "ogre." "I grasped his throat to silence him," the creature remembered, "and in a moment he lay dead at my feet."[49] After that, the creature met the servant, Justine, and decided to frame her for the murder by planting in her pocket a locket it had taken from the slain boy.

The Malignant Mate

Having finished its terrible tale, the creature turned to Frankenstein and said,

> You must create a female for me, with whom I can live in the interchange of those sympathies necessary for my being. This you alone can do; and I demand it of you as a right which you must not refuse to concede. . . . It is true, we shall be monsters, cut off from all the world; but on that account we shall be more attached to one another. Our lives will not be happy, but they will be harmless, and free from the misery I now feel. Oh! my creator . . . let me feel gratitude towards you for one benefit! . . . Do not deny me my request![50]

Frankenstein was apprehensive at the idea of unleashing another such dangerous being on the world. But he felt deeply guilty for creating the animated corpse that now stood before him, a miserable social outcast that would never know happiness. Frankenstein agreed to the creature's request on the condition that it would take its new mate and leave Europe forever.

The man then departed Mt. Blanc and returned to Geneva. There, his father urged him to fulfill Mrs. Frankenstein's dying wish and marry Elizabeth. A wedding date was set. But Victor Frankenstein did not feel comfortable starting a new life with the woman he loved before finishing the ghastly work the creature had demanded. Frankenstein had heard that a number of new discoveries had recently been made about the properties of living matter. So he set out, accompanied by his friend Henry Clerval, to tour Europe and learn whatever he could. The two men eventually traveled to London and then to Edinburgh, Scotland.

Finally, Frankenstein left Henry behind and rented a small house on a remote Scottish island. There, the reluctant labor of creating a woman for the creature would take place. But as the work proceeded and the man slowly pieced together a second body from the remnants of human cadavers, he grew increasingly hesitant.

> As I sat, a train of reflection occurred to me, which led me to consider the effects of what I was now doing. . . . I was now about to form another being.
> . . . She might become ten thousand times more malignant [evil] than her mate, and delight, for its own sake, in murder and wretchedness. . . . Had I a right, for my own benefit, to inflict this curse upon everlasting generations? . . . For the first time the wickedness of my promise burst upon me.[51]

At that moment, the creature appeared at the window. Evidently, it had been following Frankenstein during his recent journeys, watching his every move. Suddenly possessed by a surge of boldness and defiance, the man tore apart his

*The creature is enraged that Victor has destroyed the mate it longs for.
"I shall be with you on your wedding night," it warns the man.*

latest creation before the watcher's astonished eyes. The creature let out a bellow of despair and vanished. But soon it was back. "You have destroyed the work you began," it told Frankenstein.

> I have endured incalculable fatigue, and cold, and hunger; do you dare destroy my hopes? . . . Shall each man find a wife for his bosom, and each beast have his mate, and I be alone? . . . Are you to be happy, while I grovel in the intensity of my wretchedness?[52]

The creature's creator remained resolute and demanded that it leave. "It is well. I go," the thing muttered with an icy grin. "But remember, I shall be with you on your wedding night."[53] And then, before the man could stop it, it disappeared into the darkness.

Two More Murders

Not long after this disquieting episode, Frankenstein put his instruments and notes in a sack, rowed a small boat out into the sea, and dumped the contents overboard. Then, as the vessel drifted, he slept. When he awakened, he found himself near the Irish coast and went ashore. Some local people there led him to a nearby village, where the local magistrate, Mr. Kirwin, accused him of murder. A man had been found strangled, said Kirwin, and a woman who lived near the beach claimed she had seen a mysterious man rowing a small boat near the site of the murder. Kirwin led Frankenstein to the body, which lay in a room in an inn. "I entered the room where the corpse lay," Frankenstein recalled,

> and was led up to the coffin. How can I describe my sensations on beholding it? I feel yet parched with horror, nor can I reflect on that terrible moment without shuddering and agony. The examination, the presence of the magistrate and witnesses, passed like a dream from my memory, when I saw the lifeless form of Henry Clerval stretched before me. . . . The human frame could no longer support the agonies I endured, and I was carried out of the room in strong convulsions.[54]

Afterward, Victor Frankenstein remained seriously ill for two months. During that time, Mr. Kirwin nursed him back to health, and the magistrate became convinced that the man he had assumed was guilty of killing Clerval was actually innocent. Soon, Frankenstein was cleared of the charges. But the death of a third person directly or indirectly caused by his own hated creation weighed heavily on him.

Returning to Geneva, Frankenstein prepared for his wedding with mixed feelings. On the one hand, he was joyful at the prospect of joining the woman he loved in a lifelong bond. On the other, he was filled with dread that the creature would fulfill its threat and attempt to kill him on the very day of his wedding. To forestall such an event, he armed himself with a knife and two pistols. But he learned too late that he had misunderstood the creature's warning. It was not Frankenstein who was in mortal danger but his bride to be. "I continued some time walking up and down the passages of the house," he recalled,

> and inspecting every corner that might afford a retreat to my adversary. But I discovered no trace of him . . . when suddenly I heard a shrill and dreadful scream. It

Elizabeth (Helena Bonham Carter) comes face to face with the creature (Robert De Niro) on her wedding night, with disastrous results.

came from the room into which Elizabeth had retired [only moments before]. As I heard it, the whole truth rushed into my mind, my arms dropped, the motion of every muscle and fiber was suspended. . . . This state lasted but for an instant; the scream was repeated, and I rushed into the room. . . . She was there, lifeless and inanimate, thrown across her bed, her head hanging down, and her pale and distorted features half covered by her hair. . . . Could I behold this and live? . . . I fell senseless to the ground.[55]

The Chase

Elizabeth, who had been so loved by the Frankenstein family, especially by Victor, was dead. Now fearing for the lives of his remaining relatives, Frankenstein rushed to his father and brother Ernest. Thankfully they were unhurt, but upon hearing of Elizabeth's demise, the elder Frankenstein crumbled. "He could not live under the horrors that were accumulated around him," Victor recalled. "The springs of existence suddenly gave way; he was unable to rise from his bed, and in a few days he died in my arms."[56]

Afflicted by the deaths of so many loved ones, Victor Frankenstein could take no more. He vowed to find the foul fiend who had stalked his family and exact vengeance. "I was possessed by a maddening rage when I thought of him, and desired and ardently prayed that I might have him within my grasp to wreak a great and signal revenge on his cursed head."[57] Following what clues he could, the determined man tracked the creature out of Europe to the shores of the Black Sea, and from there onto the tundra plains of northern Russia. All the while, the hunted thing was well aware that its creator was in hot pursuit. It left frequent messages, carved into tree bark or stone, including "Follow me; I seek the everlasting ices of the north, where you will feel the misery of cold and frost. . . . Come on, my enemy; we have yet to wrestle for our lives."[58] As Frankenstein entered the vast frozen Arctic, he found another inscription, which read, "Prepare! Your toils only begin. Wrap yourself in furs, and provide food; for we shall soon enter upon a journey where your sufferings will satisfy my everlasting hatred."[59]

After many days of frenzied pursuit, Frankenstein finally saw his elusive prey not more than a mile ahead on the ice-covered plain. But soon the man's elation faded, for the superhuman creature widened the gap, and the great ice pack beneath Frankenstein's feet began to surge, shift, and break up. Within a day he found himself adrift on a small iceberg. And for several hours he did his best to stay alive, until at last he caught sight of Walton's vessel slowly plowing its way through the remnants of the ice pack.

Creator and Creation Meet Their End

Frankenstein's narrative ends and Walton continues with his letter to his sister, telling her what transpired next. Worried that they might not escape the bleak Arctic wilderness, the captain explains, his crew threatened mutiny unless he turned the ship around and headed back for England. Two days later, Walton agreed to do so. Shortly after that, sick and frail from his long ordeals, Victor Frankenstein died. "His voice became fainter as he spoke," Walton sadly tells Margaret.

> And at length, exhausted by his effort, he sank into silence. About half an hour afterwards he attempted again to speak, but was unable; he pressed my hand feebly, and his eyes closed forever, while . . . a gentle smile passed away from his lips.[60]

That night, as the grieving Walton prepared for bed, he heard a noise from the small room where the body of the dead man lay. Entering, the captain was astonished to see the creature standing over the remains of its creator. "Oh, Frankenstein," the monstrous being exclaimed in mournful tones.

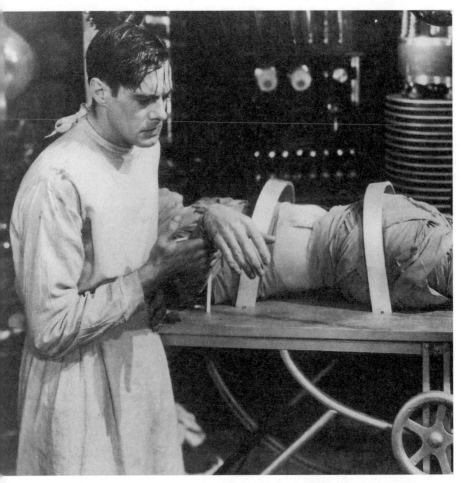

Dr. Frankenstein is pictured with the creature at the beginning of their tortured journey together. The doctor's desire to create life led ultimately to his own death.

Generous and self-devoted being! What does it avail that I now ask you to pardon me? . . . Alas, he is cold, he cannot answer me. . . . I pitied Frankenstein [and] abhorred [hated] myself. But when I discovered that he, the author at once of my existence and of its unspeakable torments, dared hope for happiness . . . then impotent envy and bitter indignation filled me with an insatiable thirst for vengeance. . . . The completion of my demoniacal design became an insatiable passion. And now it is ended; there is my last victim.[61]

Turning to Walton, the creature urged him to fear not. Only one more death would follow Frankenstein's—that of his wretched creation. The creature said it realized that it could never find either justice or happiness in the world of humans, a realm where it did not and never would belong. Instead, it planned to build a large funeral pyre and throw itself into the flames. Only then would the brutal cycle of violence be complete and the creature itself no longer haunted by the horror of its terrible deeds. The monstrous being said it looked forward to its ashes being swept away into the sea by the winds and its spirit finding peace at last.

Having said these things, Walton writes, the creature bade him farewell and suddenly jumped through the cabin window and onto a nearby iceberg. Later, the shaken man ends his last letter to his sister with the simple statement that the creature "was soon borne away by the waves, and lost in the darkness and distance."[62]

CHAPTER FOUR

The Major Characters and Their Motives

As in any story, the characters in *Frankenstein* can be considered singly and examined for their individual contributions to moving the plot along. Perhaps more important, however, is the way the major characters in Mary Shelley's great gothic tale form groups whose motives and deeds parallel and reflect on one another. All of these groups are in one way or another familial—made up either of close relatives or of circles of close friends. And during the course of the story, most of these close associations end up falling apart, mainly through the intervention of some form of untimely death.

Mary Shelley's preoccupation with these themes—family and death—reflects in large degree her own turbulent life experiences. She lived within the framework of three familial groups, all of which tragically broke down. In the first, her nuclear family, her mother died before she ever got to know her, her father was emotionally distant, and her sister committed suicide. The second group, made up of Mary and the other members of her close literary circle, was devastated by

Percy Shelley's accidental drowning. The third familial group, consisting of Mary and her own offspring, was equally crushed when three of her children died young. These disturbing events contributed to shaping Mary Shelley's psyche and outlook on the human condition. It is not surprising that she would transfer her personal disappointments and anxieties about familial relationships to the characters in her novels.

The novel Frankenstein *features several familial groups. In this scene from the 1939 film* Son of Frankenstein, *Victor's grown son (left) becomes the creature's new father figure.*

The first familial group that appears in *Frankenstein* consists of the explorer Robert Walton and his sister Margaret, the only character in the story who never actually physically appears or speaks. Walton can also be seen as a sort of father figure to the crewmen of his ship, who are dependent on him for their survival. A third group to which Walton belongs is made up of three close friends and/or sympathizers of the central character, Victor Frankenstein; the other two members are Henry Clerval and Mr. Kirwin. Victor himself is a member of the Frankenstein family—made up of the parents and three sons—which constitutes the central familial group in the story. Elizabeth, whom the Frankensteins adopt, and Justine, a family servant, can also be thought of as members of this family even though they are not related by blood. Par-

Victor (Kenneth Branagh) finds his family unit ripped apart when the creature goes on a killing spree. Mary Shelley's own familial relationships ended in tragedy.

alleling the Frankensteins is another family, the De Laceys, from whom the creature learns human language and customs. And finally, the strangest and most compelling of the novel's familial groups is that made up of Victor Frankenstein and his misshapen creation, who act out an unorthodox but very real father–son relationship, with an intense love-hate dimension. In this twisted family group, the female mate that Frankenstein attempts to make for the creature constitutes an aborted daughter-sister-wife.

These overriding familial relationships should be kept in mind while examining the following list of the novel's principal characters. (For the sake of convenience, they are listed in alphabetical order, rather than by their importance.)

Henry Clerval and Mr. Kirwin

Henry Clerval, the son of a Geneva merchant who was a close associate of the elder Frankenstein, has known Victor and Elizabeth Frankenstein since childhood, when the three played together. In his narrative to Walton, Victor draws a fond and flattering picture of Henry, describing him as

> a boy of singular talent and fancy. He loved enterprise, hardship, and even danger for its own sake. He was deeply read in books of chivalry and romance. He composed heroic songs, and began to write many a tale of enchantment and knightly adventure. He tried to make us act in plays and to enter into masquerades, in which the characters were drawn from the heroes of . . . the Round Table of King Arthur.[63]

Later, when Victor and Henry are young men, the latter follows his friend to the college at Ingolstadt. There, Henry attempts to make himself "complete master of the oriental languages. . . . He turned his eyes toward the East, as affording scope for the spirit of his enterprise."[64] It is Henry who nurses Victor back to life after he falls ill soon after bringing the creature to life. Henry is also an accomplished traveler who accompanies Victor on a European tour, which ends tragically with Henry's murder by the creature. Considering Henry's unusual intelligence, numerous talents, and unswerving loyalty, it is not difficult to understand why Victor collapses in grief when he learns of his friend's untimely death.

It is impossible to ignore the parallels between the fictional Henry Clerval and the real Lord Byron. The close friendship formed by the educated, sophisticated young trio of Victor, Henry, and Elizabeth in the book is reminiscent of the similar relationship of Percy Shelley, Mary Shelley, and Byron during Mary's late teens and early twenties. Like Henry, Byron was an avid romantic and traveler fascinated by Eastern culture. The parallel between the two men is not exact, but there is no doubt that the author drew partly on Byron's character in creating Henry.

Unlike Henry, Mr. Kirwin, a small-town Irish magistrate, was not acquainted with Victor Frankenstein in his youth. Kirwin meets Victor following Henry's murder and at first suspects Frankenstein of committing the crime. However, when Frankenstein falls ill after viewing Henry's body, Kirwin changes his mind and ends up arranging the accused man's defense. Kirwin nurses Victor back to health, just as Henry had done earlier and Walton will later, and sends for Victor's father. In Victor's view, Kirwin is a kind and benevolent man.

The Creature

Along with Victor Frankenstein, the being he created in a laboratory is one of the two central characters of the story. In later adaptations, it is often called "Frankenstein's monster" or, quite inappropriately, simply "Frankenstein" after its maker; however, in the novel, it is referred to simply as "the creature" or "the wretch." Physically speaking, it is huge, as its creator describes it "about eight feet in height and proportionally large."[65] Its skin is pale and thin, in some places

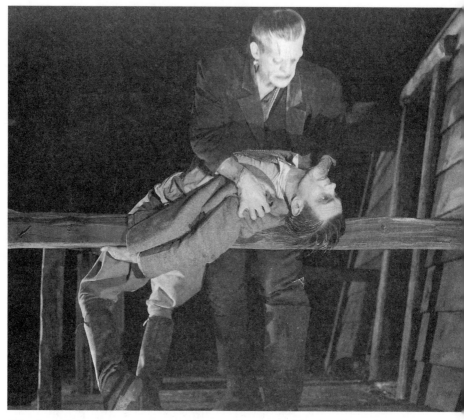

The size of Victor's monstrous creation can be seen in this photo from the 1931 film, in which the creature (Boris Karloff) clutches Frankenstein (Colin Clive).

revealing veins and arteries beneath, its hair long and matted, its face wrinkled, and its lips thin, black, and lifeless. Not surprisingly, the mere sight of the misshapen thing evokes fear and loathing in most of those who behold it.

Indeed, monstrosity and "otherness" make the creature a social outcast unable to experience normal human interaction and relationships. "All men hate the wretched," the creature tells Frankenstein. "Everywhere I see bliss from which I alone am irrevocably excluded." It insists that it is not wicked at heart and wants only to demonstrate goodwill to humans, if they will only show it some compassion and understanding.

Only repeated rejection, despair, and loneliness have driven the creature to engage in antisocial behavior. "Believe me, Frankenstein," it says,

> I was benevolent [kind]; my soul glowed with love and humanity. But am I not alone, miserably alone? You, my creator, abhor me; what hope can I gather from your fellow creatures, who owe me nothing? . . . If the multitude of mankind knew of my existence, they would do as you do, and arm themselves for my destruction. Shall I not then hate them who abhor me?[66]

The creature wants from Frankenstein only understanding and a chance for happiness normally granted by a father to his son. When its creator is unable or refuses to grant these things, it turns on him and seeks vengeance. One after another, it destroys those closest to Frankenstein, including his brother, best friend, fiancée, and father. In committing these crimes and constantly pursuing Frankenstein, the creature displays cunning, determination, and the ability to endure tremendous pain, hunger, and other hardships.

Even though the creature claims to hate Frankenstein, deep down it has familial feelings for its father figure. Indeed, when it finds the man lying dead in a cabin on Walton's ship, it expresses true and deep sadness and remorse. It realizes that by all the laws of God and humans it must be punished for what it has done to the man who gave it life and looks forward to being cleansed by a death by fire. In the end, the creature voluntarily gives up its life to atone for its sins. And in so doing, a being seen by so many as an inhuman monster attains a higher level of humanity than most people can aspire to.

The De Lacey Family

One reason that the creature displays so many human attributes is its exposure to the De Lacey family, which consists of a father (who is blind), a son named Felix, and a daughter named Agatha. For a year, the creature secretly watches them from its hiding place in a shack adjoining their humble cottage. The elder De Lacey had "silver hair and [a] benevolent countenance [look],"[67] the creature tells Frankenstein. And the son and daughter were handsome and graceful. By listening to the De Laceys, the creature learns not only human

The kindly Mr. De Lacey, head of the family the creature wants to join, was portrayed as a blind hermit in the 1935 film Bride of Frankenstein.

speech but also the breadth of human emotions, which at first seem strange and almost too intense to bear. Watching the father bestow affection on Agatha, it recalls:

> I felt sensations of a peculiar and overpowering nature. They were a mixture of pain and pleasure, such as I had never before experienced, either from hunger or cold, warmth or food; and I withdrew from the window, unable to bear these emotions. . . . What chiefly struck me was the gentle manner of these people; and I longed to join them, but dared not. . . . For the present I would remain quietly in my hovel, watching, and endeavoring to discover the motives which influenced their actions.[68]

The watching creature soon discovers the family's background and how they came to live in poverty in a remote German forest. The father

> was descended from a good family in France, where he had lived for many years in affluence, respected by his superiors, and beloved by his equals. His son was bred in the service of his country; and Agatha had ranked with ladies of the highest distinction. A few months before my arrival, they had lived in a large and luxurious city, Paris, surrounded by friends, and possessed of every enjoyment which virtue, refinement of intellect, or taste, accompanied by a moderate fortune, could afford.[69]

The De Laceys' troubles began when a Turkish merchant, the father of Safie, whom Felix loved, was unjustly arrested by the French government. They helped the man escape. But then he betrayed the De Laceys and the government imprisoned and exiled them, forcing them into their impoverished state. Safie later fled from her father and made her way to Germany to join the De Laceys.

The creature feels that it has something in common with the family. After all, both have been unfairly rejected by society and forced to live in abject poverty. Hoping to make itself known to them and perhaps join their number, the creature approaches the father and begins to explain its situation. But then Felix returns home and chases the creature away. Later, when it returns to the cottage, it finds that the family has abandoned the dwelling, most likely out of fear that the huge, misshapen intruder might return.

For the creature, the De Laceys and Safie represent the human race in microcosm. Representing two generations, both genders, and both Western and Eastern cultures and languages, they and the stories they tell display a wide range of knowledge, opinions, emotions, and experiences. Through them, the creature gains a reasonably accurate picture of the state of humanity. Moreover, their reactions to the creature—fear, rejection, and flight—typify what it, a hideous outcast, can expect from other humans it may encounter.

Elizabeth and Justine

Victor Frankenstein's adopted sister, and eventually his fiancée, Elizabeth represents to him the polar opposite of the creature. Whereas Frankenstein's creation is ugly, awkward, uneducated, and impure, Elizabeth is beautiful, graceful, educated, and pure. She and her love for the young scientist are the best things to happen to him, while the creature and its hate for its creator are the worst.

When Mrs. Frankenstein and young Victor first see Elizabeth, one of five starving children living in a hovel in an Italian forest, the young girl immediately captures their attention. "Her hair was the brightest living gold," Frankenstein later recalls,

> and, despite the poverty of her clothing, seemed to
> set a crown of distinction on her head. Her brow was

clear and ample, her blue eyes cloudless, and her lips and the molding of her face so expressive of sensibility and sweetness, that none could behold her without looking on her as a distinct species, a being heaven-sent, and bearing a celestial stamp in all her features.[70]

After joining the Frankenstein family, Elizabeth shows that her character is as admirable as her physical features. Over the years she becomes Victor's playmate, close friend, and confidant, as well as a stable anchor that balances his more volatile emotions and imagination.

Everyone loved Elizabeth. The passionate and almost reverential attachment with which all regarded her be-

Victor (Kenneth Branagh) and Elizabeth (Helena Bonham Carter) embrace. Friends since childhood, she has a calming effect on his more volatile character.

came, while I shared it, my pride and my delight. . . .
No word, no expression could body forth the kind of
relation in which she stood to me—my more than sister, since to death she was to be mine only. We were
brought up together. . . . I need not say that we were
strangers to any species of disunion or dispute. Harmony was the soul of our companionship, and the di-
versity and contrast that subsided in our characters
drew us nearer together. Elizabeth was of a calmer and
more concentrated disposition. . . . I might have become sullen in my study, rough through the ardor of
my nature, but that she was there to subdue me to a
semblance of her own gentleness.[71]

Throughout Frankenstein's endeavors at college, twisted
experiments at reanimating the dead, and early confrontations
with the creature, Elizabeth and her radiant personality remain
reassuring beacons in the man's mind. More than anything
else, Victor wants to put his monstrous experiments behind
him, marry her, and live a happy life. But this is not to be. The
creature appears on their wedding day and out of a thirst for
revenge kills Elizabeth, shattering Frankenstein's dreams.

Justine Moritz, a faithful servant to the Frankenstein family, has much in common with Elizabeth. Both are young,
beautiful, and innocent. And both suffer unjust deaths because of Victor Frankenstein's mistakes. Also, it is Elizabeth,
in a letter to Frankenstein, who supplies the details of
Justine's background:

Madame Moritz, her mother, was a widow with four
children, of whom Justine was the third. This girl had
always been the favorite of her father; but, through a
strange perversity, her mother could not endure her,
and after the death of Mr. Moritz, treated her very ill.
My aunt [Elizabeth's term of endearment for her
adoptive mother, Mrs. Frankenstein] observed this;

Seeking revenge for the misery it has suffered at the hands of its creator, the creature (Boris Karloff) attacks Elizabeth (Mae Clark) on her wedding day.

and, when Justine was twelve years of age, prevailed on her mother to allow her to live at our house. . . . My aunt conceived a great attachment to her, by which she was induced to give her an education. . . . I assure you I love her tenderly. She is very clever and gentle, and extremely pretty.[72]

Therefore, both Elizabeth and Justine are young girls who start out in unhappy family situations and end up flourishing after being taken in by the kindly Frankensteins.

Elizabeth demonstrates her almost sisterly love for Justine when she plays an active role in the young girl's defense after Justine is accused of William Frankenstein's murder. Despite these efforts, however, Justine is found guilty and executed, in large part because Victor Frankenstein does not step forward and reveal that the creature is the real murderer.

The Frankenstein Family

The Frankensteins, who generously take in Elizabeth and Justine, are a well-to-do, respected family. According to Victor, his ancestors

> had been for many years counselors and syndics [city elders and magistrates]; and my father had filled several public situations with honor and reputation. He was respected by all who knew him, for his integrity and indefatigable [untiring] attention to public business. He passed his younger days perpetually occupied by the affairs of his country; a variety of circumstances had prevented his marrying early, nor was it until the decline of life that he became a husband and the father of a family.[73]

This glowing description of Victor's father as a man of unquestioned integrity, fine reputation, and devotion to his fellow citizens creates a stark contrast with Victor himself. In the course of the story, Victor engages in questionable, ultimately disreputable and dangerous experiments that dishonor the family and threaten rather than help the community.

As for Mrs. Frankenstein, Victor relates, she was the daughter of one of the elder Frankenstein's closest friends, Mr. Beaufort. After Beaufort's death, the two were married and soon afterward she gave birth to Victor. When Victor was still a boy, Mrs. Frankenstein discovered Elizabeth and adopted her. Later, as she lies dying, Victor's mother expresses her fond desire that Victor and Elizabeth should marry. "My children," she says, my firmest hopes for future happiness were placed on the prospect of your union. This expectation will now be the consolation of your father. Elizabeth, my love, you must supply [take] my place to my younger children. Alas! I regret that I am taken from you. . . . I will endeavor to resign myself cheerfully to death, and will indulge a hope of meeting you in another world.[74]

The "younger children" Mrs. Frankenstein speaks of are Victor's brothers, Ernest and William, who were born after

Victor (Colin Clive) and Elizabeth (Mae Clark) prepare for their wedding, not realizing that the creature lurks nearby, ready to punish its creator.

Elizabeth joined the family. Ernest, seven years younger than Victor, is a gentle, fun-loving youth whom Elizabeth describes as "full of activity and spirit." The boy lacks Victor's "powers of application," she says, and "looks upon study as an odious fetter [unwelcome chain weighing him down]. His time is spent in the open air, climbing the hills and rowing on the lake. I fear that he will become an idler [lazy person]."[75] Elizabeth describes the youngest Frankenstein boy, William, as a "darling." She tells Victor that the boy "is very tall [for] his age, with sweet laughing blue eyes, dark eyelashes, and curling hair. When he smiles, two little dimples appear on each cheek, which are rosy with health."[76]

The picture the author draws of the members of the Frankenstein family as attractive, well-educated, fun-loving, and good-hearted people increases the sympathy the reader feels for them when they are destroyed by the results of Victor's experiments. Except for Mrs. Frankenstein, who dies of fever, most of the others are victims of the creature in one way or another. The creature murders William and Elizabeth; Mr. Frankenstein dies of grief upon hearing of Elizabeth's demise; and Victor dies of exhaustion while pursuing his troublesome creation. At the conclusion of the story, Ernest is the only surviving Frankenstein.

Victor Frankenstein

Though the creature causes much death and mayhem, its creator, Victor Frankenstein, is as much and probably more to blame for these ills. First, in experimenting with the secrets of life and death, the man meddles in affairs that the novel's author felt are better left to God. Second, once Frankenstein fashions the creature and gives it life, he backs away out of fear. That leaves the befuddled being alone and dependent on its instincts for survival; sooner or later, its lack of supervision and companionship are bound to cause trouble and grief for itself and those it encounters.

When Victor Frankenstein makes his first appearance in the story, he is a disheveled, exhausted, ill man who has been chasing a hated foe for many months. The Arctic explorer who finds him gives this description:

> I never saw a more interesting creature. His eyes have generally an expression of wildness, and even madness; but there are moments when, if anyone performs an act of kindness toward him . . . his whole countenance [face] is lighted up, as it were, with a beam of benevolence and sweetness that I never saw equaled. But he is generally melancholy and despairing; and sometimes he gnashes his teeth, as if impatient of the weight of woes that oppresses him.[77]

As Frankenstein begins to tell his story, it becomes clear that his wasted condition is a rather recent development. He reveals that he came from a happy, untroubled childhood. He was born in Naples, Italy, when his loving, attentive parents were visiting that romantic city.

> I remained for several years their only child. Much as they were attached to each other, they seemed to draw an inexhaustible store of affection from a very mine of love to bestow them upon me. My mother's tender caresses, and my father's smile of benevolent pleasure while regarding me, are my first recollections. I was their plaything and their idol, and something better . . . the innocent and helpless creature bestowed on them by Heaven.[78]

Only after Victor grows to young manhood, becomes interested in the secrets of life and death, and goes off to college does he leave behind his youthful state of happiness. In the next few years, the young man loses contact with his family, burying himself in what becomes an obsession to create life through artificial means. His success eventually turns to

In the 1939 film Son of Frankenstein, *the creature raises its hand, showing Frankenstein's son that his father's obsession to create artificial life has not been in vain.*

tragedy, as his creation turns on him and exacts revenge by decimating his family. This in turn instills a lust for vengeance in Frankenstein, who chases the creature to the remote Arctic wastes, where both meet their doom.

Like that of the creature, Victor Frankenstein's character is finely crafted. With much descriptive detail, Mary Shelley shows how a well-educated, happy man from a good family takes a turn onto a dark, twisted, destructive path and loses his way. Once he has "played God" and unleashed horror on the world, there is no going back; it becomes inevitable that the man will have to pay for his mistake with his own life. Still, Frankenstein, like the creature, emerges as a sympathetic character in the end. It is clear that the author, a romantic at heart, believed that God would, while forfeiting their lives, forgive both creator and creation for their transgressions.

Robert Walton

The English sea captain who is searching for a route through the Arctic to the Pacific Ocean, Robert Walton finds Victor Frankenstein floating on an iceberg and rescues him. The let-

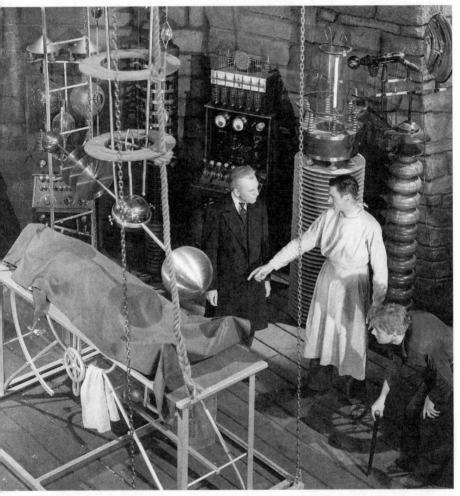

The dark and twisted path Victor Frankenstein has chosen, constituting an unhealthy perversion of science, is graphically illustrated in this photo of his lab in the 1931 film.

ters Walton writes home to his sister Margaret telling of the incident make up the body of the novel.

In his second letter, Walton describes himself and his motivations for exploration:

> I have often attributed my attachment to, my passionate enthusiasm for, the dangerous mysteries of [the] ocean, to that production of the most imaginative of modern poets. There is something at work in my soul, which I do not understand. I am practically industrious—painstaking—a workman to execute with perseverance and labor—but besides this, there is a love for the marvelous, a belief in the marvelous, intertwined in all my projects, which hurries me out of the common pathways of men, even to the wild sea and unvisited regions I am about to explore.[79]

This letter reveals that Walton has some traits in common with Victor Frankenstein. There is "something at work" in Frankenstein's soul as well. Like Walton, he longs to explore "unvisited regions." But whereas Walton's regions are geographic and quite tangible in nature, Frankenstein's lie within the more intangible workings of the life force and soul.

Walton also has something in common with the creature. Both lack a true friend. "There will be none to participate [in] my joy," says the captain. "If I am assailed by disappointment, no one will endeavor to sustain me in dejection."[80] Likewise, the creature searches for friendship but finds none. "Even [the] enemy of God and man [Satan] had friends and associates in his desolation," it points out. By contrast, "I am alone."[81] In the end, both Walton and the creature recognize Frankenstein as their only true friend. But their hopes are dashed when his untimely death leaves them as they were before this realization—alone.

CHAPTER FIVE

Major Themes Developed in the Novel

lmost two centuries have elapsed since Mary Shelley
first conceived and penned her most famous work.
Yet *Frankenstein* remains vital and widely popular.
New printed editions are published almost every year, and
fresh film versions are released on a periodic basis. Summa-
rizing the qualities that have given the novel its long life,
noted biographer Elizabeth Nitchie writes,

> [*Frankenstein*] is, to be sure, an amazing achievement
> for a girl of nineteen. But it is far more than that. It is
> no immature spinning of a "ghost story." The struc-
> ture of the plot is remarkable in its symmetrical intri-
> cacy. The characters, showing sharp contrasts with
> each other and in themselves, are convincing in their
> combination of strangeness and reality. The descriptions
> of natural scenery have a power not greatly inferior to
> that of the poets who were Mary's contemporaries
> [Percy Shelley and Lord Byron]. The novel is interest-
> ing too . . . for its reflection of the contemporary

thought in the fields of science and education, and most of all for its understanding of the tragedy of the creature who is "born with a different face," who can find no secure place in society.[82]

To this list of the book's qualities and strength, one can readily add that of skillful thematic development. The author chose more than a dozen themes, many of them basic to the human condition, and, through the words and deeds of the characters, cleverly wove them into the fabric of the story. In this way, for example, she explored the relationship between God and humanity and the consequences of humans daring

One of the main themes developed in the novel is the relationship between creator and creation, an idea derived from biblical myth as shown in the painting Adam and Eve *by Francesco Pagani.*

to usurp the deity's traditional role. To make these concepts come to life for her readers, Mary Shelley liberally borrowed ideas and situations from existing literature and mythology, chief among these Milton's *Paradise Lost* and the Prometheus myths. In her version, Victor Frankenstein assumes the roles of God and Prometheus, while the creature becomes, in a sense, a clay human, the biblical Adam, and eventually a Satanic figure. Another potent source of ideas for the novel, the steady progress of science in her day, also undergoes heavy thematic development in the book. In fact, the use and potential misuse of science, as illustrated by Frankenstein's dangerous experiments and their disastrous consequences, is unarguably the main theme of the story.

Yet there is much more to *Frankenstein* than these ideas, as substantial and fascinating as they are. Several other themes are developed more subtly but with equal facility and impact. They include, among others, the idea of life existing in some state beyond the grave, parental obligations to and nurturing of offspring, the plight of social outcasts, solitude and loneliness and the toll they take on individuals, and the power of destiny to control human affairs. Mary Shelley successfully explores these and other important themes in the novel. The result is not only a solid, complex literary framework but also characters and situations that people nearly everywhere identify with and find compelling, disturbing, or both.

Visions of Death

Certainly the possibility of life or at least some state of consciousness beyond the grave has always been one of the most compelling topics of human consideration and debate. Mary Shelley recognized that this theme was implicit in her story; after all, the being Victor Frankenstein creates is resurrected from a conglomeration of parts taken from dead bodies. In her view, failure to develop this core theme further would amount to cheating her readers. Consequently, the book is

The character of Frankenstein's mother provides the traditional religious view that in death the soul goes to heaven, as in Louis Janmot's painting The Flight of the Soul.

replete with references to death and, variously, fear of, acceptance of, or efforts to overcome and reverse death.

In real life, speculation about what happens after death is extremely varied, running the gamut from simple religious belief in an afterlife, to the conviction that nothing exists after death, to ghastly conceptions of zombies and ghouls preying on the living. Mary Shelley captured this diverse range of visions in the novel. Victor Frankenstein's mother presents the traditional religious view that family and friends will eventually be reunited in a better place. On her deathbed, she tells Victor and Elizabeth, "I will endeavor to resign myself cheerfully to death, and will indulge a hope of meeting you in another world."[83]

A more morbid and disquieting vision of life after death materializes when Frankenstein endows a heap of dead bones, organs, and skin with life. Does the creature find itself in a better place? Decidedly not, since it is an artificial creation; it has no memory of a prior life for the simple reason that it never existed before Frankenstein animated it. For the creature, therefore, what others see as a life resurrected is the only life it has ever known. Moreover, it believes that this is the only life it will ever know. Unlike the human characters, it does not foresee itself enjoying any sort of conscious state after death. In the end, it actually looks forward to death as a state of nothingness where it can finally find rest after its miserable existence on earth. "When I shall be no more," the creature tells Robert Walton as they stand over Frankenstein's body,

> the very remembrance of us . . . will speedily vanish. I shall no longer see the sun or stars, or feel the winds play on my cheeks. Light, feeling, and sense will pass away; and in this condition must I find my happiness.[84]

As for Victor Frankenstein, the fear of both death and walking dead things haunts him throughout the story. He flees in terror after witnessing the creature's first stirrings. Soon afterward, the man dreams about seeing his beloved Elizabeth turn into a zombie before his eyes. She was "walking in the streets," he recalls, and "I embraced her." But then "her features appeared to change, and I thought that I held the corpse of my dead mother in my arms." Even worse, "I saw the grave-worms crawling in the folds of the flannel."[85]

Like the creature, Victor Frankenstein at times longs to die to escape the horrendous situation in which he finds himself. Yet more often the man fights this urge, for both unselfish and selfish reasons. When he believes that the creature will try to kill him on his wedding day, he worries that his untimely passing will adversely affect his bride:

> When I thought of my beloved Elizabeth—of her tears and endless sorrow, when she should find her lover so

Victor Frankenstein chooses to live rather than kill himself because he cannot bear to think of Elizabeth (Helena Bonham Carter) enduring "endless sorrow."

barbarously snatched from her—tears . . . streamed from my eyes, and I resolved not to fall before my enemy without a bitter struggle.[86]

Later, Frankenstein more selfishly desires to avoid death because he is driven to exact revenge on the murderer of his relatives and friends. The half-crazed man begs Walton to carry on the quest to kill the creature if he, Frankenstein, should die. He seems to believe that if he and his loved ones are not avenged, he will find no rest in the afterlife. "Swear that he [the creature] shall not live," Frankenstein demands of Walton. "Swear that he shall not triumph over my accumulated woes, and survive to add to the list of his dark crimes." Walton should thrust his sword into the creature's heart, Frankenstein says. Then he adds an eerie promise to help from beyond the grave: "I will hover near, and direct the steel aright [guide the blade to its target]."[87]

Failure as a Parent

Frankenstein's hatred and pursuit of the creature in the climax of the novel is all the more remarkable when one considers that the man is in a very real sense the thing's father figure. The creature did not spring from a normal sexual union between a man and woman, but Victor Frankenstein nevertheless brought it into the world. And it began its life in much the same confused, unknowing, and needy state that human infants do. Therefore, despite the creature's unusual mode of conception and its extreme ugliness, the issue of parental nurture cannot be ignored in the story. Indeed, it is the absence of such nurture that causes much of the trouble. Abandoned at the moment of its birth by its creator-father, the creature is forced to fend for itself in a hostile world, where it learns to hate and kill.

To emphasize Frankenstein's failure as a parent and the dire consequences of that failure, Mary Shelley repeatedly shows the opposite—strong, healthy familial relationships and their importance. Young Victor, for example, came from an exceptionally loving family with a strong father figure. He tells Walton:

My parents were possessed by the very spirit of kindness and indulgence. We felt that they were . . . the agents and creators of all the many delights which we enjoyed. When I mingled with other families, I distinctly discerned how peculiarly fortunate my lot was, and gratitude assisted the development of filial love [the love of a child for its parents].[88]

The creature witnesses similar strong filial love at work in the De Lacey family, presided over by a loving, caring father. This only serves to increase its bitterness at having been abandoned by Frankenstein. The poor wretch is eventually gripped by the hope of becoming a part of the De Lacey family. "The more I saw of them," it recalls,

> the greater became my desire to claim their protection and kindness; my heart yearned to be known and loved by these amiable creatures. To see their sweet looks directed towards me with affection was the utmost limit of my ambition.[89]

Unfortunately for the creature, the De Laceys reject it and in effect it is abandoned a second time. Then it decides to seek out Frankenstein and attempt to make some kind of connection. "To whom could I apply with more fitness than to him who had given me life?"[90] However, once again the wretch finds only rejection. In the end, following Frankenstein's death, it cries out: "I, the miserable and the abandoned, am an abortion, to be spurned at, and kicked and trampled on. . . . My blood boils at the recollection of this injustice!"[91]

The Social Outcast

In fact, rejection by both individuals and society as a whole is the creature's unhappy lot throughout the story. Despite its initial innocence and good heart, its huge size and distorted features consistently instill fear in all it meets. And its alienation from humanity makes it a social outcast.

Mary Shelley begins developing this theme of alienation from the first moment the creature appears in the story. Captain Walton and his men see a huge figure moving across the ice floes in the distance. And the sight of "this apparition,"

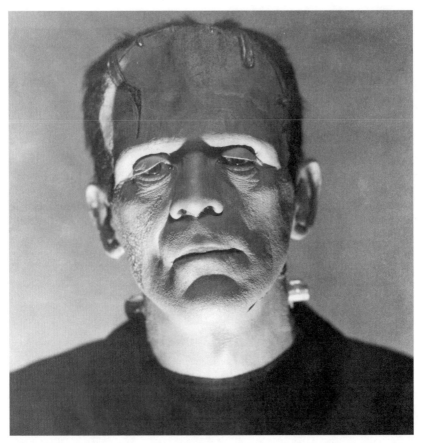

The creature's huge frame and misshapen features, wonderfully captured in Boris Karloff's makeup and performance, instill fear in nearly everyone it meets.

which "excited our unqualified wonder,"[92] immediately establishes a tone of alien mystery. Who or what could this monstrous figure be, and why is it here alone, so far removed from normal human habitations?

Later, the reader learns that the creature's alienation from people and society began even before it awakened. Frankenstein could have made the body of normal size and taken care to ensure that its features were fair and well proportioned. But in his haste and thoughtlessness, he did not. This virtually guaranteed that the creature would find it difficult, if not impossible, to fit into normal society. Also, Frankenstein not only abandons his creation, but he fails to give it a name, condemning it to begin life without a clear identity. Instead, it is called "wretch," "monster," "ogre," "fiend," and other epithets reserved for unsavory social outcasts, further reinforcing its alienation from the human race.

Later still, the creature seems to accept the reality of its rejection by society. And in exchange for Frankenstein's promise to build a female companion for it, the creature offers to reinforce its alienation by living out the rest of its days in a remote region. "If you consent," it says,

> neither you nor any other human being shall ever see us again. I will go to the vast wilds of South America. . . . We shall make our bed of dried leaves. . . . I swear to you, by the earth which I inhabit, and by you that made me, that . . . I will quit the neighborhood of man, and dwell as it may chance, in the most savage of places.[93]

But this journey never takes place. Frankenstein ends up destroying the half-finished female and he and the creature become embroiled in their final battle to destroy each other. Finally, Frankenstein dies. And this completes the creature's alienation. Despite its accumulated grievances and hatred for its creator, the creature's connection with the man was the last emotional link it had with humanity, and now that link has been severed.

The Ravages of Loneliness

Existing hand in hand with and reinforcing the motif of alienation is the equally bleak theme of solitude. From the beginning of the novel to the end, Mary Shelley explores how loneliness affects not only the creature but other characters, and always with negative results. "I have no friend," Robert Walton tells his sister in his second letter to her. A romantic adventurer at heart, Walton has gone off on a lonely quest into uninhabited regions. "I greatly need a friend," he says, "who would have sense enough not to despise me as romantic, and affection enough for me to endeavor to regulate my mind."[94] When Frankenstein appears, Walton happily believes that he has at last found the companion he had longed for. But then the other man dies, leaving the explorer once more alone and dejected.

Victor Frankenstein also spends much of his time in a state of solitude. "I was now alone," he tells Walton, recalling the weeks and months following the beginning of his studies at the college in Ingolstadt. Frankenstein admits that as a boy he had enjoyed the company of his siblings and friend Henry Clerval. But "I believed myself totally unfitted for the company of strangers." After arriving at school, he "was conducted to my solitary apartment."[95] Soon, Frankenstein is drawn in to his obsessive quest to create life artificially and steadily severs all contacts with other people. He works in total seclusion, which takes a toll on him. Later, when working on the female creature, he retreats from society once more, and his solitude begins to feel like an imprisoning force. "Chains and darkness were the only objects that pressed upon me," he remembers.

> Sometimes, indeed, I dreamt that I wandered in flowery meadows and pleasant vales [valleys] with the friends of my youth; but I awoke, and found myself in a dungeon. Melancholy followed, but by degrees I gained a clear conception of my miseries and situation. . . . During many months . . . a solitary cell had been my habitation.[96]

After the death of Clerval, Elizabeth, and others, Frankenstein withdraws from the world yet again, this time to chase the creature. The man's solitude now becomes a lonely struggle to rid the world of the menace he himself had

"A solitary cell had been my habitation," Victor Frankenstein (Kenneth Branagh) says, recalling the many lonely months he spent while constructing the creature.

earlier unleashed. By the time Walton stumbles on Frankenstein in the Arctic wastes, it appears that his lack of contact with other people has turned him into a raving madman. How else can the explorer explain the wild tale Frankenstein tells? "Are you mad, my friend?" Walton asks. "Would you . . . create for yourself and the world a demoniacal enemy [an enemy possessed by a demon]?"[97] Walton worries that the story the man has told may be nothing more than a delusion brought on by severe loneliness. "He enjoys one comfort," the explorer says,

> the offspring of solitude and delirium. He believes that, when in dreams he holds converse with his friends, and derives from that communion consolation

for his miseries, or excitements to his vengeance, that they are not the creations of his fantasy.[98]

The theme of solitude is developed in greatest detail, of course, in the creature's story. In their first meeting, on Mt. Blanc, the creature tells Frankenstein of its misery at being cut off from humanity. "Everywhere I see bliss," it says, "from which I alone am irrevocably excluded."[99] In time, these feelings cause the wretch to curse its creator. Such hatred is the natural result, the creator explains, of "the reflections of my hours of despondency and solitude."[100] When the creature finishes telling its unhappy tale to Frankenstein, the man accuses it of crimes and expresses doubt that it can be trusted. To this, the creature replies:

My vices are the children of a forced solitude that I abhor; and my virtues will necessarily arise when I live

Frankenstein (Colin Clive) and the creature (Boris Karloff) meet on a mountainside. In the novel, the creature tells its maker it has been cruelly excluded from human company.

in communion with an equal. I shall feel the affections of a sensitive being, and become linked to the chain of existence and events from which I am now excluded.[101]

Destiny's Cruel Clutches

However, the creature is not destined to feel affection, nor to find some rewarding connection with the human race. Instead, its fate is to remain alone and to carry forth its agenda of revenge against its creator. This brings the reader to one of the strongest, though also one of the most subtly interwoven, themes of the novel. All of the characters, but particularly Victor Frankenstein and his creation, seem swept along in a gruesome, destructive chain of events that none can stop or reverse. Each must move forward to meet his or her destiny, no matter how hopeless and unwanted it might be. The idea of a preordained human destiny, or fate, driven or manipulated by unseen outside forces, was (and still is) a popular theme of romantic fiction. And in the novel, Mary Shelley repeatedly reinforces the notion that no person can avoid the dictates of fate.

The theme is especially well developed in the experiences of the title character. Victor Frankenstein feels trapped in a chain of events beyond his control, almost like an actor forced to follow the script of a human drama even though he dislikes or dreads the plot twists. Frankenstein summarizes this plight to Walton when the two first meet:

> I thank you for your sympathy, but it is useless; my fate is nearly fulfilled. I wait but for one event [the destruction of the creature], and then I shall repose [rest] in peace. . . . Nothing can alter my destiny. Listen to my history, and you will perceive how irrevocably it is determined.[102]

As Frankenstein begins to tell Walton this "history," he describes how choosing to follow a specific course of study at college proved to be a major and fateful turning point in his life. It led him down the dark road to unwholesome, dangerous experiments. Moreover, from that time on he was "bound" by the hand of fate for "ruin." He could not avoid a "storm" of evil that was "hanging in the stars" (a reference to astrology, the pseudoscience in which distant heavenly bodies are purported to determine human destiny). His "guardian angel" made an effort to guide him onto a better path. But preordained fate was simply too powerful to resist. "It was the strong effort of the spirit of good," he says. "But it was ineffectual. Destiny was too potent, and her immutable laws had decreed my utter and terrible destruction."[103]

The first instance of fate leading the young man down the wrong path came when one of his professors stimulated his interest in chemistry, an understanding of which was vital to his subsequent experiments with life and death. The day this occurred "decided my future destiny," Frankenstein recalls. Later, that same destiny "led" him "to examine the cause and progress of decay," and "forced" him to visit morgues and crematoriums (facilities for burning dead bodies) to study corpses up close.[104] Cold fate had "taken an irresistible hold of my imagination."[105] A few years later, the man was devastated by the murder of his brother William, yet "I did not conceive the hundredth part of the anguish I was destined to endure."[106] Finally, having completed his narrative to Walton, Frankenstein restates his belief that he can do nothing to stop the inevitable. He would dearly like to find some higher purpose to which he might dedicate his life, "but such is not my destiny. I must pursue and destroy the being to whom I gave existence; then my lot on earth will be fulfilled, and I may die."[107]

This last phrase hauntingly mirrors the creature's final speeches to Walton in the novel's finale. The wretch announces that it will destroy itself because it "must be done." Corrupted by murder and other crimes, "where can I find rest but in death?" After all, "the bitter sting of remorse will

Actor Robert De Niro's eyes capture the tortured state of the creature as it plots to destroy is creator.

not cease to rankle in [irritate] my wounds until death shall close them forever."[108]

In the world Mary Shelley created in the book, neither the creature nor its creator could escape destiny's cruel clutches. In the real world, destiny is likely more blind and dispassionate, and most events probably happen more by random chance than by some preordained master plan. Yet it cannot be denied that it is every person's destiny to die in the end. There, in the ominous twilight of one's life, Frankenstein's world and the real world coincide. Mary Shelley recognized this fact and, despite the many fantastic aspects of her story, she carefully exploited real and universal human fears of death. She also forced her readers to confront other unpleasant but ever-present realities, including loneliness, abandonment, murder, revenge, the bizarre, and the unknown. And therein lies the enduring power of her gothic masterpiece of horror and human tragedy.

Notes

Introduction: Not One but Many Frankensteins

1. Christopher Small, *Mary Shelley's* Frankenstein: *Tracing the Myth.* Pittsburgh: University of Pittsburgh Press, 1973, p. 13.

2. Peter Hutchings, *Hammer and Beyond: The British Horror Film.* New York: Manchester University Press, 1993, p. 198.

3. Wheeler W. Dixon, "The Films of Frankenstein," in Stephen C. Behrendt, ed., *Approaches to Teaching Shelley's* Frankenstein. New York: Modern Language Association of America, 1990, pp. 178–79.

Chapter 1: The Life and Influences of Mary Shelley

4. M.K. Joseph, ed., *Frankenstein: Or, the Modern Prometheus,* by Mary Shelley. (1831 edition) New York: Oxford University Press, 1969, p. 5.

5. Anne K. Mellor, *Mary Shelley: Her Life, Her Fiction, Her Monsters.* New York: Methuen, 1988, p. 57.

6. Quoted in Mellor, *Mary Shelley,* pp. 9–10.

7. Godwin ran his own small publishing house and released Mary's volume under the imprint of the "Godwin Juvenile Library." By 1812, when she was fifteen, the verses had sold well enough to require four editions, and they were reissued once more in 1830 with illustrations by the noted artist Robert Cruikshank.

8. Quoted in introduction to Maurice Hindle, ed., *Frankenstein: Or, the Modern Prometheus,* by Mary Shelley (1831 edition). New York: Penguin Books, 1985, pp. 14–15.

9. Quoted in Frederick L. Jones, *Mary Shelley's Journal.* Norman: University of Oklahoma Press, 1947, p. 41.

10. Quoted in Donald F. Glut, *The Frankenstein Legend: A Tribute to Mary Shelley and Boris Karloff.* Metuchen, NJ: Scarecrow Press, 1973, p. 24.

11. Quoted in Muriel Spark, *Mary Shelley.* New York: Dutton, 1987, p. 154.

12. Quoted in Glut, *The Frankenstein Legend,* pp. 24–25.

13. Quoted in Spark, *Mary Shelley,* p. 57.

14. Quoted in Emily W. Sunstein, *Mary Shelley: Romance and Reality.* Boston: Little, Brown, 1989, p. 223.

15. Quoted in Mellor, *Mary Shelley*, p. 147.
16. Mellor, *Mary Shelley*, pp. 147–48.
17. Spark, *Mary Shelley*, p. 154.
18. Quoted in Joseph, ed., *Frankenstein*, p. 5.

Chapter 2: The Sources of the Ideas for *Frankenstein*

19. Quoted in Joseph, ed., *Frankenstein*, p. 10.
20. Quoted in Joseph, ed., *Frankenstein*, p. 7.
21. Quoted in Joseph, ed., *Frankenstein*, pp. 7–8.
22. Quoted in Joseph, ed., *Frankenstein*, p. 9.
23. Quoted in Joseph, ed., *Frankenstein*, p. 10.
24. Quoted in Joseph, ed., *Frankenstein*, p. 10.
25. Quoted in Joseph, ed., *Frankenstein*, pp. 13–14.
26. For these and other changes Percy Shelley made in the manuscript, see Mellor, *Mary Shelley*, pp. 59–63.
27. Quoted in Spark, *Mary Shelley*, p. 154.
28. Joseph, ed., *Frankenstein*, p. 41.
29. Joseph, ed., *Frankenstein*, p. 57.
30. Quoted in Joseph, ed., *Frankenstein*, pp. 8–9.
31. Mellor, *Mary Shelley*, p. 100.
32. Quoted in introduction to Joseph, ed., *Frankenstein*, p. viii.
33. Quoted in introduction to Joseph, ed., *Frankenstein*, pp. xiv–xv.
34. Joseph, ed., *Frankenstein*, pp. 129, 131.
35. Small, *Mary Shelley's Frankenstein*, p. 64.
36. Joseph, ed., *Frankenstein*, p. 221.

Chapter 3: The Story Told in *Frankenstein*

37. Joseph, ed., *Frankenstein*, p. 19.
38. Joseph, ed., *Frankenstein*, p. 24.
39. Joseph, ed., *Frankenstein*, p. 25.
40. Joseph, ed., *Frankenstein*, pp. 35–36.
41. Joseph, ed., *Frankenstein*, p. 45.
42. Joseph, ed., *Frankenstein*, p. 48.
43. Joseph, ed., *Frankenstein*, p. 57.
44. Joseph, ed., *Frankenstein*, p. 76.

45. Joseph, ed., *Frankenstein*, pp. 98–99.
46. Joseph, ed., *Frankenstein*, p. 99.
47. Joseph, ed., *Frankenstein*, p. 101.
48. Joseph, ed., *Frankenstein*, p. 106.
49. Joseph, ed., *Frankenstein*, pp. 142–43.
50. Joseph, ed., *Frankenstein*, p. 144.
51. Joseph, ed., *Frankenstein*, pp. 165–66.
52. Joseph, ed., *Frankenstein*, pp. 167–68.
53. Joseph, ed., *Frankenstein*, p. 168.
54. Joseph, ed., *Frankenstein*, p. 176.
55. Joseph, ed., *Frankenstein*, p. 195.
56. Joseph, ed., *Frankenstein*, p. 198.
57. Joseph, ed., *Frankenstein*, p. 198.
58. Joseph, ed., *Frankenstein*, pp. 204–205.
59. Joseph, ed., *Frankenstein*, p. 205.
60. Joseph, ed., *Frankenstein*, p. 218.
61. Joseph, ed., *Frankenstein*, pp. 219–20.
62. Joseph, ed., *Frankenstein*, p. 223.

Chapter 4: The Major Characters and Their Motives

63. Joseph, ed., *Frankenstein*, p. 37.
64. Joseph, ed., *Frankenstein*, p. 69.
65. Joseph, ed., *Frankenstein*, p. 54.
66. Joseph, ed., *Frankenstein*, pp. 99–100.
67. Joseph, ed., *Frankenstein*, p. 108.
68. Joseph, ed., *Frankenstein*, p. 108.
69. Joseph, ed., *Frankenstein*, p. 122.
70. Joseph, ed., *Frankenstein*, p. 34.
71. Joseph, ed., *Frankenstein*, pp. 35–36, 38.
72. Joseph, ed., *Frankenstein*, pp. 64–66.
73. Joseph, ed., *Frankenstein*, p. 31.
74. Joseph, ed., *Frankenstein*, p. 43.
75. Joseph, ed., *Frankenstein*, p. 64.
76. Joseph, ed., *Frankenstein*, p. 66.
77. Joseph, ed., *Frankenstein*, p. 25.

78. Joseph, ed., *Frankenstein*, p. 33.

79. Joseph, ed., *Frankenstein*, pp. 21–22.

80. Joseph, ed., *Frankenstein*, p. 19.

81. Joseph, ed., *Frankenstein*, p 221.

Chapter 5: Major Themes Developed in the Novel

82. Elizabeth Nitchie, *Mary Shelley, Author of* Frankenstein. Westport, CT: Greenwood Press, 1970, pp. 147–48.

83. Joseph, ed., *Frankenstein*, p. 43.

84. Joseph, ed., *Frankenstein*, p. 222.

85. Joseph, ed., *Frankenstein*, p. 58.

86. Joseph, ed., *Frankenstein*, pp. 168–69.

87. Joseph, ed., *Frankenstein*, pp. 208–209.

88. Joseph, ed., *Frankenstein*, p. 37.

89. Joseph, ed., *Frankenstein*, p. 132.

90. Joseph, ed., *Frankenstein*, p. 139.

91. Joseph, ed., *Frankenstein*, p. 222.

92. Joseph, ed., *Frankenstein*, p. 24.

93. Joseph, ed., *Frankenstein*, pp. 146–47.

94. Joseph, ed., *Frankenstein*, p. 19.

95. Joseph, ed., *Frankenstein*, p. 45.

96. Joseph, ed., *Frankenstein*, p. 198.

97. Joseph, ed., *Frankenstein*, pp. 209–10.

98. Joseph, ed., *Frankenstein*, p. 210.

99. Joseph, ed., *Frankenstein*, p. 100.

100. Joseph, ed., *Frankenstein*, p. 130.

101. Joseph, ed., *Frankenstein*, p. 147.

102. Joseph, ed., *Frankenstein*, p. 30.

103. Joseph, ed., *Frankenstein*, pp. 41–42.

104. Joseph, ed., *Frankenstein*, pp. 5l–52.

105. Joseph, ed., *Frankenstein*, p. 55.

106. Joseph, ed., *Frankenstein*, p. 75.

107. Joseph, ed., *Frankenstein*, p. 212.

108. Joseph, ed., *Frankenstein*, pp. 222–23.

For Further Exploration

Below are several suggestions for essays to write about Mary Shelley's *Frankenstein,* along with a related creative project.

1. In some detail, describe the setting and circumstances in which Mary Shelley originally conceived the idea that became the core of the novel. *See:* Mary Shelley's introduction to the book's 1831 edition.

2. Who were some of the scientists who influenced Mary Shelley's writing of *Frankenstein?* How did she use their ideas in the novel? What statement and warning does the book make about the uses of science? *See:* Samuel H. Vasbinder's *Scientific Attitudes in Mary Shelley's* Frankenstein; and Chapter 5, "A Feminist Critique of Science," in Anne K. Mellor's *Mary Shelley: Her Life, Her Fiction, Her Monsters.*

3. Explain what the author meant by the book's subtitle: *The Modern Prometheus.* Who was Prometheus and what did he do? How does Prometheus's story relate to the characters and events in *Frankenstein? See:* Chapter 1, "Fire from Heaven," in Don Nardo's *Greek and Roman Mythology.*

4. List some of the familial groups in the novel. To which group does Victor Frankenstein belong? How does his familial group break down in the course of the story? To which group does the creature belong? How does its group break down?

5. Trace the major events of the creature's story, as told to Frankenstein when the two meet on the slopes of Mt. Blanc. What happens in the creature's first encounter with humans? How does it learn human language and customs? Why does it seek out Frankenstein in Geneva? Why does it kill William Frankenstein? Who is charged for this murder and why?

6. The creature never receives a name. What are some of the disparaging terms used to describe it by the humans in the story? How does the lack of a name affect the creature's identity and self-image?

7. Describe the members of the De Lacey family. How does Mary Shelley use the family in the story? How is their reaction to the creature typical of the reactions of other humans?

8. Shortly after seeing the creature come to life, Victor Frankenstein has a nightmare. What happens in this dream? How does it relate to recent events in the man's life?

9. Victor Frankenstein, the creature, and the explorer Robert Walton all have in common their solitude and loneliness. Citing appropriate passages from the novel, describe why each has difficulty finding friendship.

10. How does Frankenstein fail as a father figure? Cite two other father figures in the story and tell why they are more successful.

11. One of the central themes of *Frankenstein* is the question of whether it is moral for a human being to "play God" by creating human life. This idea certainly disturbed Mary Shelley's nineteenth-century readers. A similar question of morality surrounding a cutting-edge scientific process—human cloning—disturbs many people today. Compare the arguments made by some against human cloning to the question of the morality of creating humans artificially as in the novel. Is cloning a person the same as or different from what Victor Frankenstein does? Why? *See:* Jon Turney's *Frankenstein's Footsteps: Science, Genetics, and Popular Culture;* and Chapter 6, "Playing God: Ethical and Moral Concerns About Human Cloning," in Don Nardo's *Cloning.*

12. Rent and watch the videos of the following films based on the novel: *Frankenstein* (1931), with Colin Clive as Frankenstein and Boris Karloff as the creature; *Frankenstein: The True Story* (1973), with Leonard Whiting as Frankenstein and Michael Sarrazin as the creature; and *Mary Shelley's Frankenstein* (1994), with Kenneth Branagh as Frankenstein and Robert de Niro as the creature. Briefly describe the plot of each film. All three films have some characters and situations found in the original novel; however, each alters the story to one degree or another. Which of the three films is most faithful to the book? Why? In which film is the portrayal of the creature closest to that in the novel? Boris Karloff's performance as the creature remains the most famous to date and the one against which all others are measured. How is his creature different from Mary Shelley's? Aside from the issue of faithfulness to the novel, explain why you think one of the three films is more effective than the others as a piece of entertainment. If you were given the money to produce your own film version of the novel, would you make any changes? Why or why not? If you *would* make changes, what would they be? *See:* William K. Everson's *Classics of the Horror Film;* and Donald F. Glut's *The Frankenstein Legend: A Tribute to Mary Shelley and Boris Karloff.*

Appendix of Criticism

The Novel's Three Layers

In this excerpt from the introduction to his 1969 edition of Frankenstein, *literary scholar M.K. Joseph summarizes the threefold structure of the novel's plot, commenting briefly on each of the three stories.*

Frankenstein is constructed of three concentric layers, one within the other. In the outermost layer, Robert Walton, in his letters to his sister, describes his voyage towards the North Pole and his encounter with Victor Frankenstein. In the main, middle layer, Frankenstein tells Walton how he created the monster and abandoned it in disgust, how it revenged itself by murdering all those he loved and how he finally turned and pursued it. In the very centre, the monster himself describes the development of his mind after the flight from the laboratory and his bitterness when men reject him. In spite of her inexperience, Mary Shelley uses this concentric structure with considerable subtlety.

The story of Walton's voyage to the Pole is strange but possible; it mediates by interposing a conceivable reality between us and the more strictly marvellous story of Frankenstein and his monster, which thus remains doubly insulated from everyday reality. Yet there is a parallelism of situation and a strong bond of sympathy between Walton and Frankenstein which they are quick to recognize. Walton is a solitary like Frankenstein and his obsession with the Pole answers to Frankenstein's obsession with life. . . . Walton is setting out on a process of scientific discovery at great peril to himself and others. Frankenstein's story is, in fact, narrated as a cautionary tale which serves its purpose in the end by turning Walton back to the world of normal society. . . .

At the centre of the triple structure is the story of the education of a natural man and of his dealings with his creator. . . .

The monster is essentially benevolent [kind]; but rejection by his creator and by mankind at large has made him first a fallen Adam and then a fallen Lucifer [Satan].

In the story of his experiences there are certain improbabilities and some rather obvious contrivance—the convenient chink in the wall of De Lacey's cottage, the providentially lost portmanteau [large bag] of books, the lessons to the Arab girl Safie which also serve to provide the eavesdropping monster with a kind of crash course in European civilization. These can be more easily forgiven if we take it that here, in the centre of the book, Mary Shelley is constructing something with the schematic character of a philosophic romance. The story of the monster's beginnings is the story of a child, and at the same time he recapitulates the development of aboriginal man. He awakes to the world of the senses, discovers fire and searches for food. When men reject him, he discovers society by watching the De Laceys in their cottage.

> M.K. Joseph, ed., *Frankenstein: Or, the Modern Prometheus,*
> by Mary Shelley (1831 edition). New York:
> Oxford University Press, 1969, pp. x–xii.

Shaping the Creature's Psyche

Here, from her acclaimed biography of Mary Shelley, Anne K. Mellor suggests that the author of Frankenstein *drew partially from her own experiences and feelings in shaping the creature's psyche.*

As she wrote out her novel, Mary Shelley distanced herself from her originating dream-identification with the anxious and rejecting parent and focused instead on the plight of the abandoned child. Increasingly she identified with the orphaned creature. The heart of this three-volume novel is the creature's account of his own development, which occupies all but thirty pages of the second volume of the first edition. And in this volume, Mary Shelley spoke most directly in her own voice: Percy Shelley's manuscript revisions are far less numerous in Volume II than in Volumes I or III. As she described the creature's first experiences in the world and his desperate attempts to establish a bond of affection with the De Lacey family, Mary Shelley was clearly drawing on her own experiences or emotional isolation in the Godwin household. Specific links join the creature's life to Mary Shelley's own. The creature reads about his conception in the journal of lab reports he grabbed up as he fled from Victor Frankenstein's laboratory; Mary Shelley could have read about her own conception in Godwin's Diary (where he noted the nights on which he and Mary Wollstonecraft had sexual intercouse during their courtship). . . . Both the creature and Mary Shelley read the same books. In the years before and during the composition of *Frankenstein* Mary Shelley read or reread the books found by the creature in an abandoned portmanteau—Goethe's *Werther;* Plutarch's *Lives of the Noble Romans,* Volney's *Ruins or, . . . the Revolutions of Empire,* and Milton's *Paradise Lost,* as well as the poets the creature occasionally quotes, Coleridge and Byron. Moreover, as a motherless child and a woman in a patriarchal culture, Mary Shelley shared the creature's powerful sense of being born without an identity, without role-models to emulate, without a history. The creature utters a *cri de coeur* [cry from the heart] that was Mary Shelley's own: "Who was I? What was I? Whence did I come? What was my destination? These questions continually recurred, but I was unable to solve them."

Anne K. Mellor, *Mary Shelley: Her Life, Her Fiction,*
Her Monsters. New York: Methuen, 1988, pp. 44–45.

The Creature Becomes a Satanic Figure

As explained by literary scholar Christopher Small, when the creature reads Milton's Paradise Lost, *it recognizes that it has some things in common not only with the character of Adam but with that of Satan.*

The Monster, reading *Paradise Lost* and discovering parallels, likens himself not only to Adam but to Satan: a little later he reverts to this when he finds out that Frankenstein himself had found his own handiwork not, as God did, good, but revolting. "'Accursed creator! Why did you form a monster so hideous that even you turned from me in disgust? God, in pity, made man beautiful and alluring, after his own image; but my form is a filthy type of yours, more horrid even from the very resemblance. Satan had his companions, fellow-devils, to admire and encourage him; but I am solitary and abhorred.'" The Monster is worse off than Adam, exiled from the start, and he is also a Satan, but more wretched than Milton's, who not only had his hellish host to support him, described by Milton in such grandiose terms, but was conscious also of belonging in some way, even though a rebel, within God's universe. The Monster belongs nowhere and to nobody. As the story progresses so he becomes progressively more Satanic, his powers growing to positively fiendish capacity (he is alluded to more often as "the Fiend" in the later part of the book) and his ill deeds multiplying accordingly, but also taking on some of the Luciferian majesty so striking in Milton's Satan. In his second confrontation with Frankenstein, in Orkney, he addresses him as "slave"—"'You are my creator, but I am your master,'" and threatens him: "'Beware; for I am fearless, and therefore powerful. I will watch with the wiliness of a snake, that I may sting with its venom.'" Not surprisingly, Frankenstein in reply calls him simply "Devil."

And at the end, Monster-Adam has become quite explicitly Monster-Satan. He speaks of his last murder and act of revenge, and says, "'then I was not miserable. I had cast off all feeling, subdued all anguish, to riot in the excess of my despair. Evil henceforth became my good.'" ("So farewell Hope, and with Hope farewell Fear, / Farewell Remorse: all Good to me is lost; / Evil be thou my Good," says Milton's Satan.)

The Monster is now exactly like Satan remembering his once angelic status, but unable to comprehend it: "'I cannot believe,'" he says, "'that I am the same creature whose thoughts were once filled with sublime and transcendant visions of the beauty and majesty of goodness. But it is even so: the fallen angel becomes a malignant devil.'"

Christopher Small, *Mary Shelley's* Frankenstein: *Tracing the Myth.* Pittsburgh: University of Pittsburgh Press, 1973, pp. 64–65.

Power in the Hands of Mortals

In this excerpt from her book about Mary Shelley's life and works, Betty T. Bennett says that in using the Prometheus myths the author showed the consequences of too much power in the hands of mortals.

By subtitling her novel "The Modern Prometheus" Mary Shelley configures her story in the shadow of Prometheus's act of bringing knowledge to humankind, concretizing [clarifying] the issue through examples of educational practices and their failure throughout the novel. But in her purposive transformation of the older myth of enlightenment, with its expected benefit to humanity, she has created a new and dangerous story that challenges the rationale behind Victor Frankenstein's quest and his intended "gift." In the Greek myth, the result of Prometheus's actions, like Christ's, is redemptive suffering for humanity. Frankenstein's quest, conversely, reveals itself to be more for the attainment of personal, godlike power than for societal advancement. In this reversal of expectation Frankenstein becomes the first of a number of unheroic male central figures in Mary Shelley's fiction. A failed Prometheus, he suffers not for humankind but for his own unprincipled judgment, and not willingly. This modern Prometheus, then, reduces the "heroic" act to a mocking parody of enlightenment intention and execution.

The personification of that parody is the Creature, a . . . natural savage who evolves from a condition of instinctual goodness to learned evil, mirroring a society based on fear and more a bona fide member of that society than he ever realizes. A fundamental expectation of danger and attack inherent in systems based on power leads to a prevalent fear of the other. The Creature, as constructed by Mary Shelley, is the living metaphor of that other and as such expresses the position of anyone viewed an outsider. As the Creature educates himself first through contact with nature, then through the works of [writers] Milton, Plutarch, Volney, and Goethe, and language itself, his thoughts and actions argue for the value of the Shelleys' amalgam of reason and love. When he breaks from this model and emulates the

111

power system prevalent in the nineteenth century, he, like his creator, becomes both victim and perpetuator of that system.

Frankenstein, then, may be seen as a republican form of the Prometheus myth. Power, in this telling, is in the hands of mortals, who also have the capability to bring light to their own civilization. The issue in *Frankenstein* is not, as is so often repeated in traditional religious arguments, a lesson in the dangers of the usurpation of God's domain. Rather, consistent with Mary Shelley's reformist ideology, the novel proposes that whether a Prometheus or a Frankenstein usurps power, the result may be good or evil. In questioning the very idea of power as an instrument of God, Mary Shelley suggests that unjust social conditions can be interpreted as the work not of God but rather of humanity itself and therefore are subject to change.

Betty T. Bennett, *Mary Wollstonecraft Shelley: An Introduction.* Baltimore: Johns Hopkins University Press, 1998, pp. 35–36.

The Creature's Human Will

In this insightful tract, Christopher Small suggests that leaving the creature alive at the end of the story makes the reader relate more to its plight; also, says Small, what makes the creature most frightening is its independent and unpredictable human will.

The profundity of Mary's insight, in leaving the Monster alive at the end of her tale, is not simply that the Monster as the external creation of Promethean man continues to exist and to extend his power over human life with the fatal marvels of technology. That is obvious, a continuation and extension of monstrousness in the circumstances of life which has its due reflection in the continuing life of the Frankenstein fable. The much more potent intuition of Mary, as we have seen, was to show the Monster as the projection of Frankenstein's (and Shelley's) own shadow, an internal being or psychic creation given visible shape; and thus we can see further that in leaving her story without an end she was obeying an impulse of profound mercy. For while the Monster has not yet carried out his intended self-immolation, which will be ours as well, not merely are we respited [given a break] again and again from physical destruction, though drawing nearer all the time, but we still have the chance to meet him as he truly is, a part of ourselves. He has not yet completed his task of destruction; for our part we have not even started ours, of reconciliation, but are given a continually extended stay of execution in which to come to ourselves and begin.

It is not easy. The Monster is lost in a world as desolate and trackless as the Arctic waste; it seems impossible to get in touch with him again. If he leads we can follow, but only towards nothingness and despair. Nor can any meeting be *arranged*.

All arrangements for the Monster, as attempts to manipulate what is itself a metaphor of the breakdown of manipulation, render an actual meeting more difficult. What makes the Monster so terrifying is his unpredictability and independence of human will: he is an instrument disobedient to his maker. But as an image of scientific creation in general he cannot be brought back under control by scientific means; that is only to multiply monsters or to render the Monster more monstrous. And this effect is typically to be seen in the growth of science fiction, where imagination (or more accurately, fancy) attempts to deal with the present works and future possibilities of science within scientific terms.

Christopher Small, *Mary Shelley's* Frankenstein: *Tracing the Myth.* Pittsburgh: University of Pittsburgh Press, 1973, pp. 293–94.

Visual Codes and Race Discrimination

Scholar Judith Halberstam explains how Mary Shelley often uses descriptions of the physical and racial traits of various characters to show how these characters are either accepted by society or discriminated against.

The monster in *Frankenstein* establishes visual horror as the main standard by which the monster judges and is judged. The most central episode in the novel, the narrative of the De Lacey family, establishes visual recognition as the most important code in the narrative of monstrosity. The story of the De Laceys is buried within the monster's story, their story is a subset of his, but his story (history) becomes a model of history itself as he learns of "the strange system of human society" and of "the division of property, of immense wealth and squalid poverty; of rank, descent, and noble blood."

Just as the monster reads *Paradise Lost* as "a true history," so "true history" is reduced to the story of one family at the innermost recess of the novel. True history and fiction trade places so that the story of the family replaces the story of nations; and the narrative of the body replaces the history of creation; and the significance of visual codes becomes greater than that of heritage. The fiction of the monster replaces the history of discovery and invention that first Walton and then Frankenstein try to tell. And through these series of substitutions, the "true history" of the world boils down to the monster's reading list, a quirky canon [rule] of stories for underdogs, and a tale of subjectivity as a self-knowledge that inheres to the human.

But humanity as well as monstrosity, in this novel, depends upon visual codes for its construction. The women in Victor's family, Elizabeth,

Caroline, and Justine, in their roles and fates in the novel, suggest the contradictions which lie at the heart of any attempt to distinguish definitively between human and monster. Elizabeth is rescued by Caroline from a peasant family. Caroline notices Elizabeth in the poor family's cottage because "she appeared of a different stock." Elizabeth is "thin and very fair" while the peasant children are "dark-eyed, hardy little vagrants." Indeed, it happens that Elizabeth is of "different stock" and the daughter of a nobleman, fit, therefore, for adoption. Caroline adopts Justine also but Justine must remain a servant since her heritage reveals no nobility. Birth, then, or blood rather, separates one woman from another and prepares one for marriage and the other for service. But notice that the difference between the noble and the debased is clearly exhibited in this instance upon the surface of the body—Elizabeth stands out from the rest of her poor family because she is thin and fair.

The class designation implied by "different stock," because it is a distinction based upon blood, exemplifies very well how . . . "racial discrimination" springs from the narrative. . . . Racial discrimination in *Frankenstein* [seems] to be a way of transforming class into a natural and immutable category, but as the difference in status between Elizabeth and Justine shows, the transformation is more complicated than this. By emphasizing that Elizabeth stands out from the "dark-eyed, hardy little vagrants" in the peasant family, Shelley betrays a class-biased belief that not only is nobility inherent but aristocratic class coincides with aristocratic race and is therefore *visible*. Race discrimination, indeed, displaces or at least supplements class hierarchies in this narrative partly because the theme of visible monstrosity demands that identity be something that can be seen. The monster, as we know, represents the threat not of a new class but of a new *race* of beings.

> Judith Halberstam, *Skin Shows: Gothic Horror and the Technology of Monsters*. Durham, NC: Duke University Press, 1995, pp. 38–40.

Conflict Between Masculine and Feminine

One of the more subtle themes of Mary Shelley's Frankenstein, *says scholar William Patrick Day, is a marked contrast between masculine and feminine images and social realms. Here, he describes the opposing images of masculine solitude and feminine family ties.*

The conflict between the masculine and the feminine is embodied in the opposition between male isolation and the feminine family. The three concentric rings of the novel all repeat this dynamic: Walton's rejection of his sister, Mrs. Saville and her family in England; Victor's rejection of his family, shortly after his mother's death, for six years at the university; and finally, the creature's rejection by the Delacy family. The dynamic is not, of course, quite the same in all instances: Walton and Victor have parallel experiences, while the creature reverses their pattern. Walton and Victor both leave behind the world of women in favor of those of men—the sea or the university—but the creature desperately wants to enter the world of women and the family. Strikingly, when he cannot do this, he forms a male community of two, himself and Victor, though Victor is an unwilling partner in this enterprise. The stories of all three men end in the icy polar wastes, identified as the scene of purely masculine activity—the search for power and fame—and finally the world of death.

The families in the novel all appear, at least at first, as attractive alternatives to arctic horror. The Frankensteins are close and loving, though this love is mainly showered on young Victor, who conceives of himself as the center of his family's life. Even more the quintessential feminine family are the Delacys, whom the creature watches through a chink in the wall. In his view, the Delacys are wonderfully happy, spending their whole lives loving and caring for one another. The family appears to be a safe haven, a refuge from the outside world. But these two families are literally refugees. The Delacys are outcasts, accepted neither by Christians nor Muslims, and the Frankensteins are a collection of strays. Caroline, Elizabeth, and Justine, who, though a servant, is like a member of the family, come from families that have broken up, primarily for economic reasons. The make-up of these families signals their essential weakness and the precarious place of the affectional ideal in the world. The creature yearns for a family only because he has never had one; based on their experiences, Victor and Walton both flee their families, though at the same time, each longs for that haven they have deprived themselves of, Walton by leaving it, and Victor by allowing the creature to destroy it.

William Patrick Day, *In the Circles of Fear
and Desire: A Study of Gothic Fantasy*. Chicago:
University of Chicago Press, 1985, pp. 139–40.

Transferring the Novel to Film

In this excerpt from his summary of the films made from Mary Shelley's famous novel, Wheeler Winston Dixon gives some fascinating background information about the making of the most famous Frankenstein movie—the 1931 version starring Boris Karloff.

In 1931, James Whale directed the first sound version of *Frankenstein* for Universal Pictures, under the supervision of the producer Carl Laemmle, Jr. The script of the 1951 film had a rather convoluted genesis [beginning]. The original novel was in the public domain and so could be used by anyone. Universal, however, based its version of *Frankenstein* on an Americanized version of Peggy Webling's 1930 London stage play of the novel and then brought in John L. Balderston (who had worked with Hamilton Deane in adapting his play of *Dracula* for Universal earlier in 1931) to help with the screenplay. . . . Mary Wollstonecraft Shelley does receive a credit, although it is not one that I suspect she would be overly fond of: "From the novel of Mrs. Percy B. Shelley." The finished film script has little in common with her novel, but it is still an effective, if slightly dated, piece of gothic filmmaking, highlighted by Boris Karloff's adroit [skillful] performance as the monster and by the atmospheric, forced-perspective sets used throughout the film. With this 1931 film Whale created a series of iconic [formulaic] conventions that rapidly became clichés in the decade and a half that followed and that, until the advent of the 1957 and 1976 productions, severely limited any serious approach to the novel's actual concerns.

That said, one must acknowledge the many successes of the film. Whale executes beautiful dolly or tracking-camera shots, unusual for the early sound period [early days of using sound in movies], that allow the camera to float among the actors, participating in the action it records. Karloff effectively evokes sympathy and empathy for the monster, who is not allowed a single line of dialogue and who could easily have been rendered an insensitive brute. The sets, strongly influenced by the 1919 German film *The Cabinet of Dr. Caligari,* present a nightmarish . . . backdrop for both indoor and outdoor sequences. Although there are a few genuine outdoor scenes, most of the film was shot indoors to allow Whale precise control of the lighting and sound recording. Whale also has an excellent sense of dramatic pacing, which, for the first half of the film at least, keeps the plot moving forward with grisly assurance. In the first reel, Henry Frankenstein (Victor in the novel) is a near-demonic presence, maniacally dedicated to proving his theory that he can give life to an artificially constructed human being. The first ten minutes of the film reveal that Henry is willing—even eager—to exhume [dig up] freshly buried corpses, to cut down executed criminals from the gallows, or to break into a medical school auditorium to steal a human brain, all in order to create his "child." He is assisted by Fritz, a hunchbacked halfwit ably played by Dwight Frye (who specialized in these roles; he also played the part of Renfield, Dracula's pathetic assistant, in the

1931 film version of Bram Stoker's novel). Henry cuts himself off from fiancée, father, former teachers, and friends to pursue his experiments in a lonely, ruined castle, a visually ideal location for experiments that the film represents as beyond the boundaries of acceptable scientific inquiry. Perhaps the most serious thematic deviation from the novel occurs when Fritz, sent by Frankenstein to steal a "normal, healthy brain" from the Goldstadt Medical College, bungles the assignment by dropping the normal brain and makes off with an "abnormal, criminal brain" described as exhibiting a "distinct degeneration of the frontal lobes." Because the brain comes from the skull of a brute who led a life of "violence, brutality, and murder," the unfortunate creature who receives it should be doomed to a similar existence. But Karloff's monster acts quite reasonably throughout the film, killing Fritz only after being continually tormented with a lighted torch and savagely whipped by the hunchback. The famous scene in which Karloff meets little Maria, who shows him the only kindness in the film, further demonstrates that the plot device involving the substituted brain is both unnecessary and inconsistent with the film's own action. Watching Maria throw flowers in the water, Karloff smiles and laughs for the first time in the film; when there are no more flowers to be thrown in the water, the monster reaches out to Maria in a spirit of childlike play and throws her in the water, thinking that she, too, will float. Maria drowns, of course, but her death cannot be construed as an act of violence on the monster's part. It is simply an accident that sets up the final third of the film, in which the villagers form a lynch mob to avenge Maria's death. With Henry as one of their leaders, the villagers track the monster to a windmill, which they set on fire, ostensibly killing the Creature.

Wheeler Winston Dixon, "The Films of Frankenstein,"
in Stephen C. Behrendt, ed., *Approaches to Teaching Shelley's* Frankenstein. New York: Modern Language Association of America, 1990, pp. 170–71.

Chronology

1797
Mary Godwin (later Mary Shelley), daughter of the controversial writers William Godwin and Mary Wollstonecraft, is born in London on August 30; her mother dies ten days later.

1801
William Godwin marries his neighbor Mary Jane Clairmont, whose children by a previous marriage—Charles and Jane (later called Claire)—bring the number of children in the Godwin household to four (counting young Mary's half-sister, Fanny Imlay Godwin).

1812
Mary leaves home for an extended stay at the home of a family friend, William Baxter, near Dundee, Scotland.

1814
Mary's returns to London; she befriends poet Percy Bysshe Shelley, who has recently become a regular visitor to the Godwin home; she and Percy (accompanied by Claire) run off together to the Continent (Europe) in July; they return to London in September.

1815
Mary gives birth to a daughter, who dies, unnamed, a few days later.

1816
Mary's and Percy's son William is born; Mary, Percy, William, and Claire travel to Geneva, Switzerland, in May and rent a house next door to Lord Byron, the renowned poet; Mary begins writing *Frankenstein* in June; in October, Fanny Imlay Godwin commits suicide; two months later, Percy's wife, Harriet, is found drowned; three weeks after Harriet's death, Mary and Percy are married in London.

1817
Percy Shelley loses custody of his children with Harriet; Mary finishes writing *Frankenstein* in May; in September, she gives birth to a daughter, Clara.

1818
Mary publishes *Frankenstein* anonymously in March; young Clara dies in September.

1819
In June, young William Shelley dies (of malaria or possibly cholera); Mary gives birth to another son, Percy Florence (who will become her only child to survive to adulthood), in November.

1822
The elder Percy Shelley accidentally drowns in a boating accident off the western Italian coast.

1823
The second edition of *Frankenstein* is published; the first stage adaptation of the novel, titled *Presumption: Or, the Fate of Frankenstein,* is produced; Mary collects and edits Percy's unpublished poems; she also publishes her novel *Valperga: Or, the Life and Adventures of Castruccio, Prince of Lucca,* and her short story, "A Tale of Passions."

1824
Byron dies in Greece; Mary publishes Percy's poems as *Posthumous Poems of Percy Bysshe Shelley.*

1825
Mary receives and refuses a marriage proposal from an American actor.

1826
Mary publishes her novel *The Last Man.*

1831
Mary publishes a revised edition of *Frankenstein,* appending an introduction explaining how she originally conceived the characters and central idea.

1833
Mary publishes "The Invisible Girl" and other short stories.

1835
Mary publishes her novel *Lodore.*

1836
William Godwin dies.

1837
Mary Shelley publishes her last novel, *Falkner.*

1840
Mary and her son Percy Florence visit the Continent.

1844
Mary publishes *Rambles in Germany and Italy,* about her recent travels in Europe.

1848
Percy Florence Shelley is married.

1851
Mary Shelley dies in London on February 1; her remains are buried with those of her parents.

1931
Universal Pictures releases the first film version of *Frankenstein* with sound, the first of a long and still ongoing series of movies based on Mary Shelley's novel.

Works Consulted

Some Modern Editions of the Two Texts of *Frankenstein*

Marilyn Butler, ed., *Frankenstein: Or, the Modern Prometheus,* by Mary Shelley (1818 edition). New York: Oxford University Press, 1994.

Robert E. Dowse and D.J. Palmer, eds., *Frankenstein: Or, the Modern Prometheus,* by Mary Shelley (1831 edition). New York: Dutton, 1963.

Maurice Hindle, ed., *Frankenstein: Or, the Modern Prometheus,* by Mary Shelley (1831 edition). New York: Penguin Books, 1985.

Diane Johnson, ed., *Frankenstein by Mary Shelley* (1831 edition). New York: Bantam, 1981.

M.K. Joseph, ed., *Frankenstein: Or, the Modern Prometheus,* by Mary Shelley (1831 edition). New York: Oxford University Press, 1969.

Anne K. Mellor, ed., *Frankenstein: Or, the Modern Prometheus,* by Mary Shelley (1831 edition). New York: Washington Square Press, 1995.

Walter J. Miller, ed., *Frankenstein: Or, the Modern Prometheus,* by Mary Shelley (1831 edition). New York: Signet, 2000.

Leonard Wolf, ed., *The Annotated Frankenstein,* by Mary Shelley (1818 edition). New York: Clarkson S. Potter, 1977.

Analysis and Criticism of *Frankenstein*

Stephen C. Behrendt, ed., *Approaches to Teaching Shelley's* Frankenstein. New York: Modern Language Association of America, 1990. A series of essays exploring the novel and how best to present its themes and ideas to students.

William Patrick Day, *In the Circles of Fear and Desire: A Study of Gothic Fantasy.* Chicago: University of Chicago Press, 1985. An overview of gothic literature, including Mary Shelley's *Frankenstein.*

Radu R. Florescu, *In Search of Frankenstein: Exploring the Myths Behind Mary Shelley's* Frankenstein. Jersey City, NJ: Parkwest, 1997. This well-researched book traces Mary Shelley's travels and experiences in an attempt to explain the various influences that led her to create her most famous novel.

Judith Halberstam, *Skin Shows: Gothic Horror and the Technology of Monsters.* Durham, NC: Duke University Press, 1995. A fascinating study of gothic horror novels, including *Frankenstein* and Bram Stoker's *Dracula,* and subsequent technological advances (including film) that led to further development of their characters, plots, and themes. Highly recommended.

David Ketterer, *Frankenstein's Creation:. The Book, the Monster, and Human Reality.* Victoria, British Columbia, Canada: University of Victoria Press, 1979. One of the better modern studies of the novel, its themes, and its cultural impact.

Christopher Small, *Mary Shelley's* Frankenstein: *Tracing the Myth.* Pittsburgh: University of Pittsburgh Press, 1973. In this scholarly tour de force, the author provides excellent, detailed discussions of the literary influences of the novel, including the Prometheus myths, the writings of Mary Shelley's parents, Shakespeare's works, Milton's *Paradise Lost,* and much more.

Samuel H. Vasbinder, *Scientific Attitudes in Mary Shelley's* Frankenstein. Ann Arbor: University of Michigan Research Press, 1976. A well-written exploration of the scientific influences on and themes in *Frankenstein.*

About Stage and Film Versions of *Frankenstein*

Michael Brunas et al., *Universal Horrors: The Studio's Classic Films, 1931–1946.* Jefferson, NC: McFarland, 1990. An overview of the so-called Universal horror cycle, which included several films based on Mary Shelley's *Frankenstein.*

William K. Everson, *Classics of the Horror Film.* New York: Carol Publishing, 1990. Everson describes most of the better horror films of the twentieth century, including those based on Mary Shelley's most famous novel.

Donald F. Glut, *The Frankenstein Legend: A Tribute to Mary Shelley and Boris Karloff.* Metuchen, NJ: Scarecrow Press, 1973. A commendable, detailed history of stage and film versions of *Frankenstein,* with many quotes by filmmakers and much useful commentary by the author.

Leslie Halliwell, *The Dead That Walk: Dracula, Frankenstein, the Mummy, and Other Favorite Movie Monsters.* New York: Continuum, 1986. A noted film historian and critic reviews the best horror films, including those about Frankenstein and his hideous creation. Highly recommended for movie buffs.

David J. Skal, *The Monster Show: A Cultural History of Horror.* New York: W.W. Norton, 1993. This riveting discussion of how horror films have affected modern culture, and vice versa, contains an excellent overview of how Mary Shelley's *Frankenstein* went from novel to screen.

About Mary Shelley

Betty T. Bennett, ed., *The Letters of Mary Wollstonecraft Shelley.* 3 vols. Baltimore: Johns Hopkins University Press, 1980–1988. For scholars and Mary Shelley buffs, this is the definitive primary source about her life.

Jane Dunn, *Moon in Eclipse: A Life of Mary Shelley.* London: Weidenfeld and Nicolson, 1978. A well-written synopsis of Mary Shelley's life, times, and works.

Paula Feldman and Diana Scott-Kilvert, eds., *The Journals of Mary Shelley, 1814–1844.* 2 vols. Oxford, England: Clarendon Press, 1987. Mary Shelley's diary reveals much about her own attitudes and literary likes and dislikes, as well as those of Percy Shelley and other people close to her.

Anne K. Mellor, *Mary Shelley: Her Life, Her Fiction, Her Monsters.* New York: Methuen, 1988. A richly detailed, extremely well written biography of Mary Shelley, with much analysis of her works, including her less well-known novels. Highly recommended for those interested in the subject.

Emily W. Sunstein, *Mary Shelley: Romance and Reality.* Boston: Little, Brown, 1989. One of the better recent biographies of Mary Shelley.

About the Society and Literature of Mary Shelley's Era

Marilyn Butler, *Romantics, Rebels, and Reactionaries: English Literature and Its Background, 1760–1830.* New York: Oxford University Press, 1981. Discusses the revolutionary writers of the generation before Mary Shelley (including her parents), as well as her own, and the influences these writers had on her and her works.

Msao Miyoshi, *The Divided Self: A Perspective on the Literature of the Victorians.* New York: New York University Press, 1969. A scholarly study of Victorian literature.

Philip A.M. Taylor, ed., *The Industrial Revolution in Britain: Triumph or Disaster?* Boston: D.C. Heath, 1958. A collection of scholarly essays exploring the issue of the rise of science and industry in Britain in the 1700s and 1800s.

G.M. Young, *Portrait of an Age: Victorian England.* London: Oxford University Press, 1973. A well-written, informative synopsis of life in England in the nineteenth century.

Other Works Relating to *Frankenstein* and Mary Shelley

Betty T. Bennett, *Mary Wollstonecraft Shelley: An Introduction.* Baltimore: Johns Hopkins University Press, 1998.

Kenneth N. Cameron, ed., *Romantic Rebels: Essays on Shelley and His Circle.* Cambridge, MA: Harvard University Press, 1973.

Paul Cantor, *Creature and Creator: Mythmaking and English Romanticism.* New York: Cambridge University Press, 1984.

Edward Edelson, *Great Monsters of the Movies.* Garden City, NY: Doubleday, 1973.

Donald F. Glut, *The* Frankenstein *Catalogue: Being a Comprehensive Listing. . . .* Jefferson, NC: McFarland, 1984.

Roy Huss and T.J. Ross, eds., *Focus on the Horror Film.* Englewood Cliffs, NJ: Prentice-Hall, 1972.

Peter Hutchings, *Hammer and Beyond: The British Horror Film.* New York: Manchester University Press, 1993.

James F. Iaccino, *Psychological Reflections on Cinematic Terror: Jungian Archetypes in Horror Films.* Westport, CT: Praeger, 1994.

Frederick L. Jones, *Mary Shelley's Journal.* Norman: University of Oklahoma Press, 1947.

Robert Kiley, *The Romantic Novel in England.* Cambridge, MA: Harvard University Press, 1972.

George Levine, *The Realistic Imagination: English Fiction from* Frankenstein *to* Lady Chatterly's Lover. Chicago: University of Chicago Press, 1981.

W.H. Lyles, *Mary Shelley: An Annotated Bibliography.* New York: Garland, 1975.

John McCarty, *The Modern Horror Film: 50 Contemporary Classics.* New York: Carol Publishing, 1990.

Don Nardo, *Cloning.* San Diego: Lucent Books, 2002.

——— *Greek and Roman Mythology.* San Diego: Lucent Books, 1998.

Elizabeth Nitchie, *Mary Shelley, Author of* Frankenstein. Westport, CT: Greenwood Press, 1970.

Harold Perkin, *The Origins of Modern English Society, 1780–1880*. London: Routledge and Kegan Paul, 1973.

Mary Shelley, *Rambles in Germany and Italy, in 1840, 1842, and 1843*. 2 vols. London: Edward Moxon, 1844.

Muriel Spark, *Mary Shelley*. New York: Dutton, 1987.

J.L. Talmon, *Romanticism and Revolt: Europe 1815–1848*. New York: Harcourt, Brace, and World, 1967.

Malcolm I. Thomis and Peter Holt, *Threats of Revolution in Britain, 1789–1848*. London: Macmillan, 1977.

Mary K.P. Thornburg, *The Monster in the Mirror: Gender and the Sentimental/Gothic Myth in* Frankenstein. Ann Arbor: University of Michigan Research Press, 1987.

Jon Turney, *Frankenstein's Footsteps Science: Genetics, and Popular Culture*. New Haven, CT: Yale University Press, 1998.

William Veeder, *Mary Shelley and* Frankenstein: *The Fate of Androgyny*. Chicago: University of Chicago Press, 1986.

William A. Walling, *Mary Shelley*. New York: Twayne, 1972.

Susan Wolstenholme, *Gothic (Re)Visions: Writing Women as Readers*. Albany: State University of New York Press, 1993.

Index

Picture Credits

About the Author

Classical historian and literary scholar Don Nardo has written
or edited numerous books about the lives, works, and characters of great English writers, among them Shakespeare,
Chaucer, Dickens, J.R.R. Tolkien, and H.G. Wells. His study
of Shakespeare's *Hamlet* for the Understanding Great Literature series has received widespread acclaim. Mr. Nardo lives
with his wife, Christine, in Massachusetts.